NASHVILLE
Like a Local

NASHVILLE
Like a Local

BY THE PEOPLE WHO CALL IT HOME

Contents

NIGHTLIFE

OUTDOORS

meet the locals

BAILEY FREEMAN

Bailey has called Nashville home for six years, but has lived a stone's throw from Music City pretty much her whole life. When she's not writing about her favorite places, Bailey is likely found on an art crawl, defying gravity as an aerial acrobat, and attending as many concerts as is humanly possible.

KRISTEN SHOATES

Writer and brand strategist Kristen moved to Nashville on a whim ten years ago and has never looked back. Outside of trying new restaurants – an occupational hazard of travel writing – Kristen is reading in coffee shops, hiking another trail, and hanging out in rock clubs with her guitar-playing husband.

Nashville

WELCOME TO THE CITY

Music legacies don't come more iconic than Nashville's – it's this inimitable heritage that ultimately earned Nashville its nickname "Music City." But when it comes to art and originality, Nashville doesn't just stop at music. Creativity really does fuel this place. You'll see it in the hopeful young songwriters and leather-clad veteran pickers harmonizing on live music stages, the pigment-splashed artists painting bright shocks of art across public walls, and the budding chefs turning to their grandma's recipe books to reimagine Southern favorites.

We can't forget that Nashville bears the scars of a painful past, but from the darkness emerged a powerful Civil Rights movement and a progressive, forward-looking community. After all, this is a place that's long existed as a crossroads, bringing together people of every background and passion to create a place that's truly extraordinary.

And that's not hyperbole. Nashville is chaotic good. It defies expectations and takes everyone along for the ride. Here, quiet dinners end in head-banging, art gallery tours in karaoke singalongs. And that's where this book comes in. We've rounded up the places that stay true to Nashville's creative, energetic, and unpredictable heart, from the quirky rooftop bars that locals will wait all week for to the electric venues that nurture established and new talent. Of course, there are more Nashvillians than these pages can do justice to. Instead, this book celebrates snapshots of local life in a city that's as diverse as its inhabitants.

Whether you're a Nashvillian wanting to dig deeper into your hometown, or a visitor looking to tap into Nashville's one-of-a-kind tune, this book will help you embrace a lesser known Nashville. Find the rhythm behind Music City, the local way.

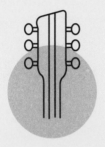

Liked by the locals

"In Nashville, you're constantly
surrounded by dream chasers,
whether they've lived here 20 years
or two. You can't help but feel
inspired – you're in a place where
beauty is created all the time in so
many different ways. It's a privilege
to be part of the audience."

BAILEY FREEMAN, WRITER

Something is always afoot in Music City. Think alfresco concerts in spring and summer (and beyond), football playoffs in fall, and festive fun in winter.

Nashville
THROUGH THE YEAR

SPRING

OUTDOOR CONCERTS
As things start to warm up, locals have one thing in mind: live music in the great outdoors. Stages pop up across the city, with Musicians Corner, in Centennial Park *(p171)*, the focal point in May.

IROQUOIS STEEPLECHASE
Nashvillians don their finest attire and most flamboyant hats for a day of horse racing and tailgating at Percy Warner Park, where it's more about mingling than actually betting.

TIN PAN SOUTH
Captive audiences flock to bars and venues for this songwriters' festival, which is all about the art of the writers' round.

FASHION FORAYS
Designers show off their new collections at Nashville Fashion Week, while those who can't make it to the runway hit patios in jazzy shirts and sundresses.

SUMMER

AQUATIC ADVENTURES
With the humidity rising, locals gravitate toward the city's lakes for a cooling dip or a bit of leisurely canoeing, drink in hand (also known as "cabrewing").

FESTIVAL FUN
It wouldn't be Music City without festival season. In June, country music fans make for the CMA Music Festival and wannabe flower children gather for boho Bonnaroo. Then, in July, the Ryman

(p116) hosts Bluegrass Nights before locals wave goodbye to summer (for free) at Live on the Green in early September.

STREET FAIRS

Locals love a summertime street fair. East Nashville celebrates avant garde art at the Tomato Arts Festival; SoBro offers up Music City Brewer's Fest; and the whole city is decked out with rainbow flags for July's Pride celebrations.

FALL

HARVEST TIME

Weekends revolve around corn mazes and pumpkin patches out in rural Tennessee – as if locals needed another excuse to throw on checkered flannel.

FOOTBALL FOR DAYS

Sports bars fill up with the first kickoff of the season. Though college football is king, Nashvillians love cheering on the Titans and telling themselves that this is finally the year they'll make the playoffs.

CULTURAL CELEBRATIONS

With the days cooling off, locals head indoors for a dose of culture. Film fans descend on big venues and little pop-ups to watch screenings as part of Nashville Film Festival, while all-round artsy people can't get enough of Artober, a month-long gala of visual and performing arts.

WINTER

HOCKEY HULLABALOO

Southerners and hockey might not sound like they go together but Nashville Predators fans are some of the rowdiest and, during the winter season, their cries of support are heard throughout town.

HOLIDAY CHEER

Favorite Christmas flicks are screened in movie theaters, lights are draped around the city, and locals take to the Opryland Hotel ice rink. It's the same every year and the locals just love it.

THE OPRY AT THE RYMAN

Country music concert the Grand Ole Opry returns to its home of the Ryman from December for a run of winter shows, much to the delight of Nashvillians.

COZY INDOORS

As things cool off, locals migrate inside for a glass of red in a cozy bar or, if it's abnormally cold, movie night at home.

There's an art to being a Nashvillian, from the do's and don'ts in a bar to negotiating the city's busy streets. Here's a breakdown of all you need to know.

Nashville
KNOW-HOW

For a directory of health and safety resources, safe spaces, and accessibility information, turn to page 190. For everything else, read on.

EAT
Nashvillians love to dine out and, handily, Music City has got more restaurants than they can shake a drumstick at. Weekends revolve around sociable brunches and hearty Southern lunches, with spots filling up from 10am. Some places shut in the afternoon to switch up the vibe before the dinner crowd arrives from 5pm, though most locals eat after 6pm. Whatever the hour, it's a good idea to have a reservation.

DRINK
Cafés are a huge part of daily life in Nashville – songwriting wouldn't happen without the aid of coffee. As for alcohol, the city's drinking scene is big business, starting with happy hour specials and ending when bars close, often as late as 3am. And yet, in spite of the universal presence of alcohol in Nashville, it's illegal to take drinks out onto the street. Most bars will split checks for individual bills, but if you start a tab be sure to close it – some bars add a fee if you forget. A final heads-up: drinks Downtown are much pricier than in the rest of the city.

SHOP
The good people of Nashville prefer to support small creators (of which there are many) and generally avoid chain stores and malls. Shops open around 10 or 11am and close at 5 or 6pm (some close earlier from Monday through Wednesday). It's always worth carrying a tote; there isn't a charge for a plastic bag but you'll find Nashville warmly welcomes eco warriors.

ARTS & CULTURE

Music City's museums aren't cheap to enter, with many charging at least $20. Some good news: a lot of galleries offer free entry, which comes in handy on weekends when various organized art crawls take place. Music and performing arts venues vary hugely in price but, compared to the likes of NYC, tickets are affordable (you can see a rising band for just $35). It's all pretty casual, but you might want to dress up a bit for the ballet or theater.

NIGHTLIFE

A typical night out in Nashville revolves around music bars – this is Music City, after all. Even those heading to a concert will first hit a music bar for pre-drinks. Downtown parties hard, especially on Broadway (aka Honky Tonk Highway), so you'll likely see a fair bit of drunkenness here. Thankfully, the rest of the city is more judicious with its alcohol intake. Going-out attire is casual, though some ritzier bars do have a dress code so check ahead. Whatever you're wearing, don't forget to have your ID on you.

OUTDOORS

On sunny days, Nashvillians flock to the city's parks for picnics and catch-ups. Here there are countless bins, so do your bit to help look after these green spaces (Tennessee also has various laws for littering, and you can be fined). If you're outside in summer, be sure to carry sunscreen and plenty of water; the sun is at its hottest in July and August.

Bear in mind

Here are some more tips and tidbits that will help you fit in like a local.

» **Keep cash handy** The majority of places take card but some small, down-home spots remain cash-only so have some dollars to hand.

» **No smoking** Smoking is banned inside, though some late-night bars bend this rule. Don't follow suit; if you have to light-up, do it outside.

» **Always tip** Adding at least 18 percent to your restaurant bill is a must. It's also polite to tip musicians and bartenders ($1 per beer; more if it's a cocktail).

» **Stay hydrated** You'll find drinking fountains in parks, and waitstaff are great at offering tap water.

GETTING AROUND

A hodgepodge of established and newer, scrappier neighborhoods (p14), Nashville is in fact home to fewer than a million people – surprising for a state capital. It's anchored by the North, South, East, and West Nashville neighborhoods, with Downtown its midpoint and the Cumberland River looping through the northeast (separating East Nashville from its siblings). It's not the easiest city to navigate; the roads that run parallel to the Cumberland (from Downtown to West Nashville) are kind of gridded, but those running perpendicular to the river are named. In a nutshell: it's confusing.

So, to make your life easier we've provided what3words addresses for each sight in this book, meaning you can quickly pinpoint exactly where you're heading with ease.

On foot

Its layout might be a bit of a puzzle but Nashville is best explored on foot; you'll be helping the environment and get to see the city in all its glory, too. Some parts of town do lack sidewalks (it's been an issue for decades) so be vigilant. Southern folk walk as they live – at a laid-back pace – so don't shadow them impatiently. They're also friendly, neighborly people 'round these parts so feel free to say hello if you are bypassing. And if you need to stop and check a what3words location, step aside so locals can mosey along on their way.

On wheels

Nashville is one of the South's most bike-friendly cities, with numerous locals choosing to pedal to work. It's a good workout: Nashville is a hilly city, and what may start as a casual cycle can quickly ascend into a challenging, uphill pedal. But traveling on wheels is still a great way to soak up the scenery. Bike lanes are mainly found around Downtown, so take care if you're heading beyond the area. Be sure to also follow all the rules of the road, such as obeying traffic signals, signaling when turning, and giving way to pedestrians. Tennessee law requires cyclists to use reflectors and a front white light when riding. If using headphones, keep one ear free. And always wear a helmet. No arguments.

The city's official bikeshare program, Nashville BCycle, rents bikes from its various docking stations for one day ($5) or 7 days ($10). But there's a catch: the pass covers 60-minute trips, so you need to "clock in" at a station every hour or you'll incur a charge. It's worth it for the freedom, though.

By public transportation

Nashville's public transit system, which is run by the Metropolitan Transit Authority (MTA), mainly comprises buses (the addition of a light rail network has been hotly debated for years). If we're honest, the network isn't always the most efficient way of getting around; schedules aren't regular, so if you miss your ride you'll be waiting half an hour to an hour for the next bus to appear, and some routes don't run on weekends or holidays. You also need to pay your fare in cash. All this said, buses are cheap, with one journey costing just $2 and an all-day pass $4.

By car or taxi

Music City is heavily reliant on cars, with most locals driving their own wheels during the day and making use of cabs and rideshares – like Uber and Lyft – on nights out. There are some drawbacks, like heavy traffic and eye-wateringly expensive parking (Downtown, we see you). But rideshares are well developed and a reliable way to get around the city.

Looking to hire a car? Nashville's got loads of outlets to choose from. A word to the wise: traffic gets especially unruly during NFL games (the stadium is right next to the highway), so check the Titans' schedule and plan your journey carefully.

Download these

We recommend you download these apps to help you get about the city.

WHATWORDS

Your geocoding friend

A what3words address is a simple way to communicate any precise location on earth, using just three words. ///bared.oval.valve, for example, is the code for the entrance of Marathon Music Works. Simply download the free what3words app, type a what3words address into the search bar, and you'll know exactly where to go.

BCYCLE

Your local bikeshare scheme

The app for Nashville's BCycles helps you find docking stations, easily pay for your ride, and get directions to your destination.

It's Nashville's neighborhoods – each with their own character and community – that give the city its small town feel. Here we look at some of our favorites.

Nashville
NEIGHBORHOODS

12 South

Formerly the sleepy haunt of retirees, this teeny tiny 'hood is now the turf of young families and liberal yuppies, who spend their weekends on 12 South's eponymous street, browsing its boutiques and stopping for coffee. *{map 4}*

Berry Hill

Forget Music Row: it's all about Berry Hill these days. It's trendy, innovative, and fast becoming a music hub in its own right thanks to its clutch of indie recording studios. *{map 4}*

Downtown

Music City's beating heart is a hive of activity. Tourists throng in its iconic museums, buskers play for anyone who'll listen, and good-timers flock to Honky-Tonk Highway for a night of boot scootin' fun. *{map 1}*

East Nashville

Separated from the rest of the city by the Cumberland River, hipster HQ East Nashville has gentrified in the last decade, forcing out lower income families. That said, it's still loved for its cocktail bars, vintage stores, and record shops. *{map 3}*

Germantown

The clue's in the name: Germantown was founded by German immigrants, who settled here in the 1800s. These days Nashville's oldest 'hood is known for its fab dining scene. *{map 2}*

Green Hills

Only big-name musicians and rich folk can afford to live in the million-dollar mansions of Music City's priciest neighborhood. But we can look. *{map 5}*

The Gulch

With its high-rise condos and rooftop bars, the Gulch stands out against Nashville's small town charm. But what it lacks in village vibes it makes up for in chic spots for dinner and drinks, making the area a go-to at night. *{map 1}*

Hillsboro Village

A lovely little stretch of shops and cafés, Hillsboro Village has a bohemian, beatnik feel, though in truth it's the hangout of trust-funded students from Belmont and Vanderbilt universities. Gentrification has also cast a shadow over the village, with locals fighting hard against development. {map 5}

Melrose

A stone's throw from creative Berry Hill is laid-back Melrose. The neighborhood flies under the radar despite its nifty antique shops and cozy restaurants. {map 4}

Midtown

When the free, single, and ready to mingle want a wild night on the town (but not Downtown wild) they make for Midtown, where patio bars host first-rate DJs. {map 2}

Music Row

It might be the historic hub of Nashville's famous music industry but Music Row has a surprisingly down-home feel. Okay, locals don't actually live here but they do work the ol' 9 to 5 in the record labels, studios, and publishing houses that occupy the district's buildings. {map 5}

The Nations

Once a center of industry, the Nations epitomizes the city's creative character. Shabby-chic spaces house exciting breweries and cool start-ups, tempting young professionals to put down roots in the area. {map 5}

North Nashville

Black history is woven into every brick and beam in North Nashville: it was here that Fisk University (p120) opened for the education of Black students in 1866, and residents played an integral role in Nashville's Civil Rights movement. Today the area is a treasure trove of Black-owned businesses. {map 2}

SoBro

Short for "South of Broadway," SoBro is the grittier and – let's be honest – cooler sister of Downtown. SoBro comes alive at night, as locals stream into its many bars and restaurants. {map 1}

South Nashville

A multicultural area, with the largest Kurdish community in the US (affectionately called

"Little Kurdistan" by locals), South Nashville is a foodie Shangri-La. {map 4}

Sylvan Park

Everyone seems to know each other in this leafy, community-minded outpost. It's no wonder families long to live in Sylvan Park – even its name is charming. {map 5}

Wedgewood-Houston

Okay, the nickname "WeHo" might be a bit cringe but Wedgewood-Houston is seriously cool (and giving East Nashville a run for its money on the hipster scale). Edgy and unpretentious, the patch is awash with craft distilleries, art galleries, and cocktail bars. {map 4}

West Nashville

Encompassing the areas that aren't Sylvan Park and The Nations, West Nashville is largely residential with a mix of new builds and ranch houses. There's a slower pace of life here; laid-back locals while away their afternoons in chilled bars and garage-restaurants. {map 5}

Nashville
ON THE MAP

Whether you're looking for your new favorite spot or want to check out what each part of Nashville has to offer, our maps – along with handy map references throughout the book – have got you covered.

6

TN-12

Cumberland River

WHITE
BLUFF

I-40

BELLEVUE

PASQUO

I-40

FAIRVIEW

| 0 kilometers | 5 |
| 0 miles | 5 |

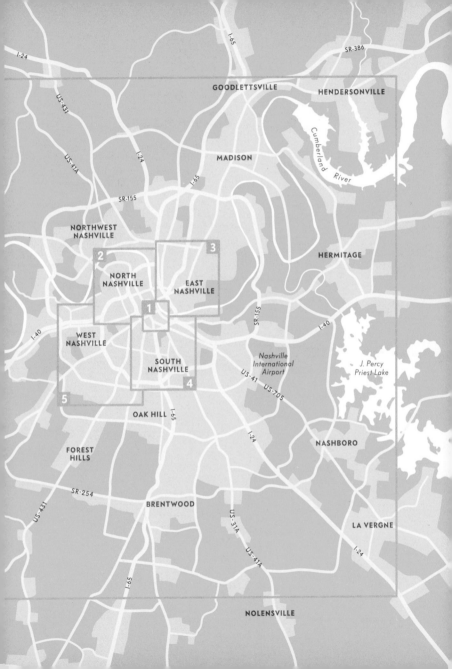

ROSA L. PARKS BOULEVARD

REP. JOHN LEWIS WAY NORTH

3RD AVE NORTH

Public Square Park

Cumberland River

Nissan Stadium

Tennessee State Capitol

CHARLOTTE AVENUE

EAST BANK

Bobby Hotel

21c Museum Hotel

Tennessee Performing Arts Center

The Arcade

Bourbon Street Blues and Boogie Bar

NORTH GULCH

One day, I will rescue your brother too

Rare Bird

Alley Taps

Bowie's

B. B. King's

Puckett's

United Street Tours

George Jones

Wildhorse Saloon

CHURCH STREET

8TH AVENUE NORTH

10TH AVENUE NORTH

Nashville Public Library

Downtown Presbyterian Church

DOWNTOWN

Robert's Western World

The Ryman

The Stage on Broadway

BROADWAY

Acme Feed & Seed

Headquarters Beercade

Tootsie's Orchid Lounge

Goo Goo Cluster

National Museum of African American Music

Nudie's Honky Tonk

Johnny Cash Museum

Ascend Amphitheater

1ST AVE SOUTH

Tennessee Sports Hall of Fame

Schermerhorn Symphony Center

BROADWAY

11TH AVENUE

12TH AVENUE SOUTH

Frist Art Museum

Country Music Hall of Fame

4TH AVE SOUTH

Hatch Show Print

VETERANS BOULEVARD

DEMONBREUN STREET

SOBRO

6TH AVE SOUTH

KOREAN

REP. JOHN LEWIS WAY SOUTH

Martin's Bar-B-Que Joint

L27 Rooftop Lounge

Bar Sovereign

The Listening Room Café

What Lifts You

THE GULCH

Cannery Row

8TH AVE SOUTH

LAFAYETTE STREET

4TH AVE SOUTH

Station Inn

L.A. Jackson

Third Man Records

City Winery

Rudy's Jazz Room

Arnold's Country Kitchen

6TH AVE SOUTH

DIVISION STREET

Carter Vintage Guitars

Tennessee Brew Works

0 meters   300
0 yards   300

MAP 1

1

E EAT

Arnold's Country Kitchen *(p36)*

Hermitage Cafe *(p35)*

Husk *(p47)*

Martin's Bar-B-Que Joint *(p39)*

Puckett's *(p37)*

D DRINK

Acme Feed & Seed *(p71)*

Alley Taps *(p76)*

Bar Sovereign *(p77)*

Bobby Hotel *(p71)*

Crema Coffee *(p80)*

George Jones *(p71)*

L27 Rooftop Lounge *(p68)*

L.A. Jackson *(p69)*

Rare Bird *(p68)*

Tennessee Brew Works *(p63)*

S SHOP

Carter Vintage Guitars *(p109)*

Goo Goo Cluster *(p96)*

Hatch Show Print *(p89)*

Third Man Records *(p108)*

A ARTS & CULTURE

21c Museum Hotel *(p130)*

The Arcade *(p128)*

Country Music Hall of Fame *(p117)*

Downtown Presbyterian Church *(p122)*

Frist Art Museum *(p126)*

Johnny Cash Museum *(p117)*

Nashville Public Library *(p123)*

National Museum of African American Music *(p116)*

One day, I will rescue your brother too *(p132)*

The Ryman *(p116)*

Schermerhorn Symphony Center *(p136)*

Tennessee Performing Arts Center *(p137)*

Tennessee Sports Hall of Fame *(p127)*

United Street Tours *(p121)*

What Lifts You *(p134)*

N NIGHTLIFE

3rd & Lindsley *(p163)*

Ascend Amphitheater *(p161)*

B. B. King's *(p155)*

Bowie's *(p153)*

Bourbon Street Blues and Bougie Bar *(p154)*

Cannery Row *(p160)*

City Winery *(p154)*

Headquarters Beercade *(p156)*

The Listening Room Café *(p155)*

Nudie's Honky Tonk *(p146)*

Pinewood Social *(p156)*

Rudy's Jazz Room *(p152)*

The Stage on Broadway *(p144)*

Station Inn *(p154)*

Robert's Western World *(p146)*

Tootsie's Orchid Lounge *(p144)*

Wildhorse Saloon *(p145)*

Ⓐ Family Matters

CLARKSVILLE PIKE

CASS STREET

ROSA L PARKS BOULEVARD

VANTAGE WAY

I-65

Ⓔ Big Al's Deli

NORTH NASHVILLE

BUCHANAN STREET

ED TEMPLE BOULEVARD

Willie B's **Ⓓ**

Ⓔ The Southern V

Ⓐ Elephant Gallery

Slim & Husky's Pizza Beeria **Ⓔ**

Rocky's Wing Shack **Ⓔ**

Bearded Iris Brewing **Ⓓ**

Butchertown Hall **Ⓔ**

Barista Parlor **Ⓔ**

Rolf & Daughters **Ⓔ**

City House **Ⓓ Ⓔ**

ABEDNEGO **Ⓢ Ⓔ**

3RD AVE NORTH

GERMAN-TOWN

Henrietta Red

DR D B TODD JR BOULEVARD

Tennessee State Museum **Ⓐ**

HEIMAN STREET

STREET

I-40

JEFFERSON ST

Jefferson Street Sound **Ⓐ**

Ⓐ One Drop Ink

Nashville Farmers' Market **Ⓢ Ⓢ**

Batch **Ⓐ**

Riddim N Spice **Ⓔ**

Fisk University **Ⓐ**

Bicentennial Capitol Mall State Park

Fisk University Galleries **Ⓐ**

Bang Candy Company

Corsair Distillery **Ⓓ**

Tennessee State University

Hadley Park

HADLEY PARK

HERMAN STREET

Marathon Music Works **Ⓢ Ⓢ**

Antique Archaeology

Nelson's Green Brier Distillery **Ⓓ**

Marathon Village **Ⓢ**

WATKINS PARK

I-40 I-65

CLIFTON AVENUE

CHARLOTTE AVENUE

Suzy Wong's House of Yum

Chauhan Ale & Masala House **Ⓔ**

Play Dance Bar **Ⓝ**

HiFi Clyde's **Ⓝ**

Tribe **Ⓝ Ⓝ**

MIDTOWN

Nashville Frontrunners **Ⓞ Ⓝ**

Canvas Lounge

BROADWAY

Adele's **Ⓔ**

Ⓝ Two Bits

Ted Rhodes Park

Cumberland River

BUENA VISTA PIKE

0 meters 800
0 yards 800

MAP 2

EAST TRINITY LANE

Grimey's **S** **D** Walden

Fox Bar &
Cocktail Club

Kernels Gourmet
Popcorn **S**

CAHAL AVENUE

E Coneheads
D Retrograde

DOUGLAS AVENUE

Black Shag Vintage **S**

CLEVELAND
PARK

Cleveland
Park

GREENWOOD AVENUE

Shugga Hi
E Bakery and Café

Pearl Diver **D**

EASTWOOD

CLEVELAND STREET

A Red Arrow Gallery

E Red Headed
Stranger

Pharmacy Burger
Parlor and **D**
Beer Garden

S The Bookshop

EASTLAND AVE

Rosepepper
Cantina **E**

McFerrin
Park

Star Struck **S**
Vintage

Graze **E**

Dolly Parton
The 5 Spot **N** **A**
S The Hip Zipper

Duke's **D**

S The Good
Fill

D Urban Cowboy

Attaboy

QDP at **D**
Butcher & Bee **E** **E** **N** Basement
East

S Fanny's House
of Music

N Lipstick
Lounge

GreKo Greek **E**
Kitchen

E
Yeast
Nashville

Honeytree
Meadery

E Wild Cow

East Nashville
Farmers' Market **S**

EAST
NASHVILLE

S Olive & Sinclair
Chocolate Co.

SHELBY AVENUE

SHELBY
HILLS

Kayak
down the
Cumberland

Cumberland
Park

DAVIDSON STREET

John Seigenthaler
Pedestrian Bridge

Music
City Flea **S**

Cumberland River

DOWNTOWN

0 meters   800
0 yards   800

MAP 3

Mitchell Delicatessen **E**

3

D Southern Grist

Vinyl **S** **E** Cafe Roze
Tap

S Whiskey Water

S Apple & Oak

Shelby Park

O Shelby Bottoms Greenway

E EAT

Butcher & Bee *(p44)*

Cafe Roze *(p35)*

Coneheads *(p49)*

Graze *(p42)*

GreKo Greek Street Food *(p54)*

Mitchell Delicatessen *(p51)*

Red Headed Stranger *(p51)*

Rosepepper Cantina *(p54)*

Shugga Hi Bakery and Café *(p33)*

Wild Cow *(p40)*

Yeast Nashville *(p34)*

D DRINK

Attaboy *(p67)*

Duke's *(p79)*

Fox Bar & Cocktail Club *(p64)*

Pearl Diver *(p67)*

Pharmacy Burger Parlor and Beer Garden *(p75)*

Retrograde *(p81)*

Southern Grist *(p61)*

Urban Cowboy *(p75)*

Walden *(p79)*

S SHOP

Apple & Oak *(p89)*

Black Shag Vintage *(p100)*

The Bookshop *(p90)*

East Nashville Farmers' Market *(p106)*

Fanny's House of Music *(p110)*

The Good Fill *(p90)*

Grimey's *(p110)*

The Hip Zipper *(p100)*

Honeytree Meadery *(p96)*

Kernels Gourmet Popcorn *(p98)*

Music City Flea *(p105)*

Olive & Sinclair Chocolate Co. *(p97)*

Star Struck Vintage *(p101)*

Vinyl Tap *(p110)*

Whiskey Water *(p94)*

A ARTS & CULTURE

Dolly Parton *(p134)*

Red Arrow Gallery *(p129)*

N NIGHTLIFE

The 5 Spot *(p153)*

Lipstick Lounge *(p150)*

QDP at Basement East *(p151)*

O OUTDOORS

Cumberland Park *(p169)*

John Seigenthaler Pedestrian Bridge *(p174)*

Kayak down the Cumberland *(p179)*

Shelby Bottoms Greenway *(p173)*

DOWNTOWN

THE GULCH

NAPIER

Pecker's Bar and Grill **N**

EDGEHILL

Rose Park

Adventure Science Center **A**

Fort Negley **A**

Barcelona Wine Bar **E**
Billy Reid **S** **D** Old Glory

Nashville Craft Distillery

Zeitgeist Art Gallery **D** **A**
E
Dozen Bakery

Jackalope **D** **D** Bastion
Gabby's **E** **D** **D** Never Never
Burgers
Humphreys
Diskin **D** Street Coffee
Cider

Fork's Drum Closet **S**

WEDGEWOOD-HOUSTON

Rumble Seat Music **N** **S** **The Basement**

Nashville Flea Market **S**

WEDGEWOOD AVENUE

Pre to Post Modern **S**

The Smiling Elephant **E** **E** Hattie B's

Savant Vintage **S**
Vinnie Louise **S**
Josephine **E**
D 12 South Taproom

Santa's Pub **D**

Tempo **D**

SOUTH NASHVILLE

Frothy Monkey **D** 12 SOUTH
Imogene + Willie **S** **S** Draper James
A I Believe in Nashville

MELROSE
M.L. Rose **D** **N** Melrose Billiard Parlor

White's Mercantile **S** **E** Epice

KIRKWOOD AVENUE

O Sevier Park

BERRY HILL
Nashville Jam Company **S**

Merengue Cafe **E**
E Sunflower Café

WOODMONT BOULEVARD

THOMPSON LANE

Paddywax Candle Bar **S**

0 meters 800
0 yards 800

MAP 4

 EAT

Barcelona Wine Bar *(p45)*
Dozen Bakery *(p32)*
Epice *(p52)*
Gabby's Burgers *(p48)*
Hattie B's *(p37)*
House of Kabob *(p53)*
Josephine *(p46)*
Merengue Cafe *(p52)*
The Smiling Elephant *(p53)*
Sunflower Café *(p42)*

D DRINK

12 South Taproom *(p72)*
Bastion *(p65)*
Diskin Cider *(p74)*
Frothy Monkey *(p82)*
Humphreys Street Coffee *(p82)*
Jackalope *(p60)*
M.L. Rose *(p74)*
Nashville Craft Distillery *(p63)*
Never Never *(p73)*
Old Glory *(p66)*
Santa's Pub *(p77)*
Tempo *(p81)*

S SHOP

Billy Reid *(p94)*
Draper James *(p93)*
Fork's Drum Closet *(p111)*

Imogene + Willie *(p92)*
Nashville Flea Market *(p107)*
Nashville Jam Company *(p99)*
Paddywax Candle Bar *(p88)*
Phonoluxe Records *(p109)*
Pre to Post Modern *(p101)*
Rumble Seat Music *(p111)*
Savant Vintage *(p103)*
Vinnie Louise *(p93)*
White's Mercantile *(p91)*

A ARTS & CULTURE

Adventure Science Center *(p125)*
Fort Negley *(p122)*
I Believe in Nashville *(p132)*
Zeitgeist Art Gallery *(p129)*

N NIGHTLIFE

The Basement *(p160)*
Melrose Billiard Parlor *(p159)*
Pecker's Bar and Grill *(p148)*

O OUTDOORS

Sevier Park *(p171)*

MAP 5

5

White Limozeen
D

WEST END AVENUE

Patterson House
D

E Tavern

Kung Fu **N** Saloon

Historic **A** RCA Studio B

MUSIC ROW

21ST AVE SOUTH

16TH AVE SOUTH

Hillsboro Village Dragon **A**

D Fido

Proper **E** Bagel

BELMONT

BELMONT BOULEVARD

I-440

E EAT

AVO *(p42)*
Kokos Ice Cream *(p41)*
Proper Bagel *(p34)*
Tavern *(p33)*
Woodlands *(p41)*

D DRINK

8th & Roast *(p81)*
The Centennial *(p76)*
Fido *(p82)*
Greenhouse Bar *(p79)*
Patterson House *(p66)*
SandBar *(p73)*
White Limozeen *(p69)*

S SHOP

ABLE *(p94)*
L&L Marketplace *(p107)*
OAK Nashville *(p90)*
Thistle Farms *(p91)*
The Turnip Truck *(p97)*

A ARTS & CULTURE

Belcourt Theatre *(p139)*
Darkhorse Theater *(p136)*
Hillsboro Village Dragon *(p133)*
Historic RCA Studio B *(p118)*
Nashville Opera *(p139)*

Off the Wall Nashville *(p133)*
The Parthenon *(p124)*
Silo Mural *(p134)*

N NIGHTLIFE

The Bluebird Cafe *(p163)*
Exit/In *(p161)*
Kung Fu Saloon *(p159)*
The Local *(p153)*

O OUTDOORS

Centennial Park *(p171)*
Love Circle *(p168)*
McCabe Park *(p169)*

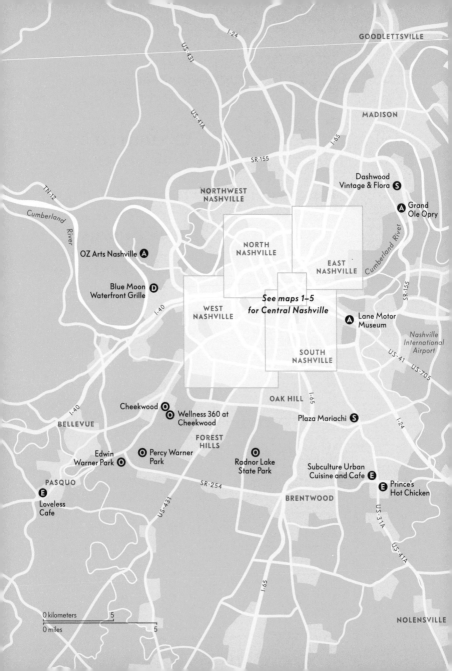

GOODLETTSVILLE

MADISON

I-24

US-431

US-41A

SR-155

I-65

Cumberland River

TN-12

NORTHWEST NASHVILLE

Dashwood Vintage & Flora **S**

A Grand Ole Opry

OZ Arts Nashville **A**

NORTH NASHVILLE

EAST NASHVILLE

Cumberland River

Blue Moon Waterfront Grille **D**

See maps 1–5 for Central Nashville

I-40

WEST NASHVILLE

SR-155

A Lane Motor Museum

Nashville International Airport

SOUTH NASHVILLE

US-41

US-70S

OAK HILL

I-65

Cheekwood **O**

O Wellness 360 at Cheekwood

Plaza Mariachi **S**

I-24

BELLEVUE

FOREST HILLS

I-40

Edwin Warner Park **O**

O Percy Warner Park

O Radnor Lake State Park

Subculture Urban Cuisine and Cafe **E**

E Prince's Hot Chicken

PASQUO

SR-254

BRENTWOOD

US-31A

US-41A

E Loveless Cafe

US-431

I-65

0 kilometers   5

0 miles   5

NOLENSVILLE

MAP 6

HENDERSONVILLE

Cumberland River

6

HERMITAGE

⊙ Stones River
Greenway

I-40

↓ Percy
Priest Lake

Swim in Percy
Priest Lake

⊙   **⊙**

Stand-up
paddle boarding

NASHBORO

I-24

E EAT

Loveless Cafe *(p39)*

Prince's Hot Chicken *(p36)*

Subculture Urban Cuisine
and Cafe *(p46)*

D DRINK

Blue Moon Waterfront
Grille *(p74)*

S SHOP

Dashwood Vintage & Flora *(p103)*

Plaza Mariachi *(p106)*

A ARTS &
CULTURE

Grand Ole Opry *(p118)*

Lane Motor Museum *(p124)*

OZ Arts Nashville *(p139)*

O OUTDOORS

Cheekwood *(p170)*

Edwin Warner Park *(p173)*

Percy Warner Park *(p172)*

Radnor Lake State Park *(p174)*

Stand-up paddle boarding *(p176)*

Stones River Greenway *(p172)*

Swim in Percy Priest Lake *(p179)*

Wellness 360 at Cheekwood *(p179)*

EAT

Classic home-cooked food (hello, hot chicken), incredible veggie fare, and globally inspired dishes keep locals well-fed. And all are served with a dollop of Southern hospitality.

Breakfast and Brunch

Roll up for a casual breakfast at a local coffee shop (yoga pants totally acceptable) or put on your Sunday best for a leisurely midday brunch with friends.

ADELE'S

Map 2; 1210 McGavock Street, The Gulch; ///attend.mole.search; www.adelesnashville.com

With a menu inspired by recipes from chef Jonathan Waxman's mom (ten points if you can guess her name), Adele's is all about splashing out on a fancy, seasonal brunch. Head here on a warm day, when the old garage doors are rolled up and groups congregate on the patio, to kick off the weekend with brioche French toast and mimosas.

DOZEN BAKERY

Map 4; 516 Hagan Street #103, Wedgewood-Houston; ///shaky.beans.stump; www.dozen-nashville.com

Forget showy or cutesy confections. Dozen is all about simple, perfectly toasted breads and flaky, buttery pastries. And, unlike other bakeries in town, there are loads of seats (though few power outlets if you're

Come early to snag some bread, then walk over to Reservoir Park to enjoy an alfresco DIY breakfast.

wanting to get that report done). The best spot? Out on the patio, where couples and their doggos soak up vitamin D with a morning coffee and croissant.

SHUGGA HI BAKERY AND CAFÉ

Map 3; 1000 Dickerson Pike, East Nashville; ///owls.loans.fans; www.shuggahibakeryandcafe.com

Splashed with turquoise on the outside and bedecked with artsy portrait paintings inside, Shugga Hi feels energetic and welcoming. Families and friends meeting for leisurely brunches pack into the cozy dining room to enjoy the weekly jazz brunch and fun creations like the Tater Tot Waffle (a French vanilla waffle topped with savory tots for the perfect crunch), or a slice of house-made pie in unconventional flavors like peach mimosa.

TAVERN

Map 5; 1904 Broadway, Midtown; ///again.school.fluid; www.mstreetnashville.com

Tavern sets the (high) bar for Nashville brunch; the Midtown staple does breakfast classics like eggs Benedict and huevos rancheros with panache, plus playful dishes like red velvet waffles. If you're feeling social, settle in at the sunny bar to wash everything down with 2-for-1 cocktails (and mocktails) alongside a genial Sunday Funday crowd.

» Don't leave without ordering some maple fondue for the table, which comes with fresh fruit, waffles, and grilled sausage. Heaven.

PROPER BAGEL

Map 5; 2011 Belmont Boulevard, Belmont; ///hangs.clown.cotton;
www.properbagel.com

You might have to throw some elbows to get into this place on a
weekend morning, but braving the line of neighborhood regulars
and Belmont students is worth it. This trendy bagel shop is run by
the Speranza family, New York transplants who have been in the
bagel business since the 1970s – and, boy, do they know their stuff.
Expect perfect bagels, house-made cream cheeses, and classic
smoked-fish sandwiches that'll transport you to the East Coast.

YEAST NASHVILLE

Map 3; 805 Woodland Street #300, East Nashville; ///lawn.melon.shut;
www.yeastnashville.com

It's all about the Tex-Czech-style *kolache* at this down-to-earth spot.
Similar to brioche, these sweetbreads are gloriously pillowy and
filled with sweet fruit, cheese, or even spiced meats. Pair with an
espresso and you've got the perfect grab 'n' go morning treat.

Try it!
MAKE PANCAKES

Relive Saturday mornings as a kid, when
you and your mom would make pancakes,
with the Pfunky Griddle. Choose your mix-ins
and make your own stack on the tabletop
griddle (*www.thepfunkygriddle.com*).

CAFE ROZE

Map 3; 1115 Porter Road, East Nashville; ///party.loft.hunter;
www.caferoze.com

Perhaps this place doesn't look like much but push through the doors and you'll see why the cool kids love this all-day café. Cafe Roze is ideal social media fodder, with pink accents and marble counters, and the food is just as elegant. Bowls of berry-flecked granola are savored by neighbors sitting up at the bar and reading the paper. At the café tables, stylish 20-somethings snap pictures of their perfectly poached eggs. It's almost too pretty to eat (who are we kidding?).

» Don't leave without trying one of the non-alcoholic coolers, made with ingredients like matcha, ginger, and turmeric – the perfect, guilt-free accompaniment to brunch.

HERMITAGE CAFE

Map 1; 71 Hermitage Avenue, Downtown; ///slows.gladiators.worry;
www.hermitage-cafe.com

Hermitage's slogan says it all: "Sobering up Nashville's wild life since 1990." Music City's night owls and early birds love this diner, which is light on frills but big on flavors. The café opens at 10pm, welcoming revelers in the early hours of the morning with plates of French toast and glasses of iced tea. Come 8am and things are more buttoned up, but the grill artists behind the counter continue to whip up preemptive hangover cures (eggs, sausage, homemade biscuits and gravy) and coffee is poured by the bucket. By noon, the diner closes its doors and takes a well-deserved break before starting afresh that evening.

Southern Staples

Southern food is rich in flavor and culture, and it's always made with love. Whether it's soul food, or BBQ, or the famously fiery hot chicken, one thing is certain: you won't go hungry in Nashville.

ARNOLD'S COUNTRY KITCHEN

Map 1; 605 8th Avenue South, SoBro; ///pasta.ruler.dating; www.arnoldscountrykitchen.com

Think of Arnold's like your middle school cafeteria, except it doesn't smell and the lunch lady is way more motherly. This is a classic "meat 'n' three" where, as you go down the line, you'll choose your favorite home-cooked meat and three sides from a selection of rotating staples (classics include: mac 'n' cheese, mashed potatoes, candied yams). The place is an institution; you've got to come here.

PRINCE'S HOT CHICKEN

Map 6; 5814 Nolensville Pike, South Nashville; ///curry.patio.moons; www.princeshotchicken.com

Nashville's famous hot chicken – crispy fried chicken coated in spicy oil and seasoning – originated here in the city's most hallowed chicken shop. Legend has it that back in the 1930s a slighted girlfriend of one Thornton Prince (a handsome farmer) sought her revenge by making Prince's chicken fiery hot. Alas, he enjoyed it so much that he turned it into a business. Today his great niece – and a Nashville icon – Ms. André Prince Jeffries continues his legacy.

PUCKETT'S

Map 1; 500 Church Street, Downtown; ///guides.squad.count; www.puckettsgro.com

As a general rule, when it comes to Southern food, the humbler the beginnings the better the food tastes. That's why no one is surprised that Puckett's, which began as a grocery store in a 1950s gas station, is one of the best places in town. Families religiously gather here for cherry wood-smoked ribs, shrimp and grits, and peach cobbler, all of which is served up with a generous side of Southern hospitality.

HATTIE B'S

Map 4; 2222 8th Avenue South, Melrose; ///crazed.bucked.film; www.hattieb.com

Prince's might be the hot chicken blueprint but Hattie B's made it a Nashville attraction. The Melrose digs tempts folks from miles around, all wanting to test their mettle against Hattie B's spicy recipes. Heat levels range from Southern (which has no spice) to "Shut the Cluck Up" (eye-wateringly spicy). After you've numbed your senses, head outside for a sweet tea and game of cornhole with the locals.

» Don't leave without ordering a side of the pimento mac 'n' cheese – a Southern twist on a homestyle classic.

Solo, Pair, Crowd

When you're in the South, you're always home. So, whoever you're with, take a seat and enjoy a warm welcome.

FLYING SOLO
Fall in love with biscuits
The South and biscuits go together like, well, biscuits and gravy. Pull up to the counter at Biscuit Love, chat with the staff, and try this fluffy Southern favorite covered in sweet or savory toppings.

IN A PAIR
Winner winner chicken dinner
Bolton's Spicy Chicken & Fish claims the hottest hot chicken in town. Challenge a friend to a mouth-melting meal and see who can better handle the heat.

FOR A CROWD
Pass the potatoes, please
Gather with a group for a family-style meal at Monell's, located in a beautiful brick Victorian in one of Nashville's oldest neighborhoods. Pass around the cornbread, fried chicken, and banana pudding like you would during Sunday dinner.

ROCKY'S WING SHACK

Map 2; 1601 9th Avenue North, North Nashville; ///cubes.socket.chief;
www.rockyswingshack.com

Demone "Rocky" Harland is a bit of a local legend. He started his
catering business out of his mom's kitchen and, after becoming a
beloved figure of local block parties, he set up this restaurant. His aim?
To nourish the community with soul food. He succeeded; hungry
pilgrims come from miles around to sample his perfect crispy wings.
» Don't leave without trying the strawberry kick. This delicate sauce
makes every flavor in the wing sing.

LOVELESS CAFE

Map 6; 8400 TN-100, Pasquo; ///referral.retained.freckled;
www.lovelesscafe.com

Lon and Annie Loveless opened this café to greet those coming in
and out of town back in 1951, and today the landmark café is still
serving up homey, Southern-style food. The biscuits – savory scones
to the uninitiated – are famous 'round these parts.

MARTIN'S BAR-B-QUE JOINT

Map 1; 410 4th Avenue South, Downtown; ///saving.items.begun;
www.martinsbbqjoint.com

Melt-in-your-mouth pulled pork? Check. Smoky, tender ribs? Check.
Savory, saucy wings? Check. This mainstay is a carnivore's dream.
Join rambunctious cowboy-booted tourists in the leafy beer garden
for an evening of bone cleanin' and, if you time it right, live music.

Veggie and Vegan

Sure, Southern cuisine is known for its liberal use of meat, butter, and cheese, but Nashville won't leave veg-lovers hungry. As for you carnivores: the veggie and vegan scene just might surprise you.

THE SOUTHERN V

Map 2; 1200 Buchanan Street, North Nashville; ///farm.sheet.poems; www.thesouthernv.com

Vegan Southern food sounds like an oxymoron but Southern V's talented husband-and-wife team, Tiffany and Clifton, have embraced the challenge and come out victorious. This sunny restaurant offers plant-based takes on favorites, like chicken and waffles, BBQ, and – of course – hot chicken, all washed down with a technicolor selection of smoothies. Homestyle cooking never felt so good.

WILD COW

Map 3; 1100 Fatherland Street, Suite 104, East Nashville; ///tapes.spoon.enable; www.thewildcow.com

Thinking of converting to the meat-free way of life? Wild Cow is great for plant-based newbs and vegan veterans alike. Why? Well, the hippie-dippie eatery makes vegan and veggie versions of international favorites, so you know what you're letting yourself in for. Chipotle seitan tacos or vegan BLT sandwiches, anyone? All ingredients are locally grown and usually organic, too.

» **Don't leave without** trying the buffalo beans and greens. The combination of the garlicky kale and the buffalo sauce is something you never knew you needed.

WOODLANDS

Map 5; 3415 West End Avenue, West Nashville; ///tests.feed.teach;
www.woodlandstennessee.com

Woodlands has been serving plant-based Indian cuisine since 2004, long before an influx of trendy vegan joints started to pop up across the city. Okay, the setting is a bit offbeat (it's beneath an old condo complex) but the food is second to none. Crispy cauliflower fritters, rava masala, coconut curry – we could go on.

KOKOS ICE CREAM

Map 5; 3 City Avenue Suite 700, West Nashville; ///tune.loops.remote;
www.kokos-ice-cream.square.site

If you're dairy-free these days and think that ice cream is a thing of the past, you're in – quite literally – for a treat. Kokos serves 100 percent plant-based ice cream with fun flavors like lavender, purple rose lemonade, and piña colada. The vegan desserts are just so pretty, as is the scoop shop's locale – a tropical-themed storage container with a sprawling patio. It's the perfect spot for a summer evening under the stars, cone in hand.

GRAZE

Map 3; 1888 Eastland Avenue, East Nashville; ///leads.things.dices; www.grazenashville.com

The sister restaurant of the uber successful Wild Cow, Graze has a modern bistro vibe. It's an any-time-of-day place; mornings see brunch squads dig into biscuits and gravy and breakfast burritos, before families arrive for an early dinner of quesadillas and mac 'n' "chorizo." Hearty portions and Southern flavors make this vegan joint a must.

AVO

Map 5; 3 City Avenue #200, Sylvan Park; ///inner.boom.dime; www.eatavo.com

Avocados and millennials really do go hand-in-hand. Take AVO, a favorite of young people who flock to this trendy outpost for its avocado margaritas and 100 percent vegan and kosher menu. And with dishes made from unprocessed ingredients, what's not to love?
» Don't leave without ordering the raw pad thai, made with zucchini noodles and peanut sauce, and topped with coconut flakes.

SUNFLOWER CAFÉ

Map 4; 2834 Azalea Place, Berry Hill; ///likely.lakes.cases; www.sunflowercafenashville.com

A haven for those with diet restrictions, Sunflower Café is rustic, humble, and plates up everything with a dollop of cheeriness. Ask to be seated outside so you can make like a plant and photosynthesize while you tuck into the garlic mushroom burger or Thai ginger bowl.

Liked by the locals

"What we strive for at Sunflower Café is giving people some peace of mind about what they order – whether they're after meat-free, soy-free, gluten-free, or oil-free."

ASHLEE CHAFFEE, FRONT-OF-HOUSE MANAGER
AT SUNFLOWER CAFÉ

Special Occasion

Best friend's birthday? Date night? Looking for an
excuse to put on a cute outfit? Nashville's got countless
memorable dining experiences to mark any occasion.
And, surprise! They won't blow your budget either.

BUTCHER & BEE

Map 3; 902 Main Street, East Nashville; ///struck.patrol.sweat;
www.butcherandbee.com

Internationally inspired small plates are passed around animated
groups of friends at Butcher & Bee, with each recipient inhaling
the mouthwatering scents of saffron aioli, chickpeas stewed in
green harissa, and perfectly succulent scallops. The jubilant feast
is paused only to clink glasses of wine (Israelian syrah, anyone?)
before the dance of the dishes resumes once more.

CITY HOUSE

Map 2; 1222 4th Avenue North, Germantown; ///warm.bonus.flank;
www.cityhousenashville.com

Ask the locals where to head for a special life event and many will
say City House. It could be credited with starting Nashville's
high-end culinary revolution since its opening back in 2007, and

If you're more of a fly-by-the-seat-of-your-pants person, you can sit up at the counter without a reservation.

James Beard Award-winning chef Tandy Wilson continues to turn out beautiful Italian fare with a Southern twist. Reservations are an absolute must.

BARCELONA WINE BAR

Map 4; 1200 Villa Place, Suite 110, Edgehill; ///haven.mess.sudden; www.barcelonawinebar.com

It's true that Spanish tapas aren't that common in the US but, praise be, Barcelona delivers that dose of the Iberian Peninsula that you've been craving. Tuck into delicious and authentic tapas that won't leave you needing to unbutton your jeans when you're done (nor tighten your wallet for the rest of the month). And ask to sit up at the marbled bar – the perfect spot to toast an occasion with a glass of rioja.

» Don't leave without sampling the grilled octopus – charred on the outside and perfectly tender on the inside. Magical.

ROLF & DAUGHTERS

Map 2; 700 Taylor Street, Germantown; ///link.raves.kind; www.rolfanddaughters.com

If you're looking for somewhere that's special without being too try-hard, Rolf & Daughters is the place for you. Based in a historic factory, the space is all brick and warm woods. But it's the menu that's the main draw; hyper-seasonal ingredients are used to craft modern pasta dishes. So don't expect to find your favorite dish a second time – you'll just have to find an excuse to return and see what's new.

BUTCHERTOWN HALL

Map 2; 1416 4th Avenue North, Germantown;
///slang.whites.influencing; www.butchertownhall.com

The style at this modern BBQ spot is showy, with food cooked on
a huge open-hearth fire, but the vibe is chilled. Inspired by Texan
meat markets, the menu is a glorious lineup of oak-smoked brisket,
pulled-pork tacos, and ember-charred vegetables. And, unlike other
spots that serve quality meat, Butchertown Hall is very affordable
so dinner doesn't come at the cost of your entire paycheck.

SUBCULTURE URBAN CUISINE & CAFE

Map 6; 5737 Nolensville Pike, South Nashville; ///hoping.flat.locate;
www.subculturecafe.com

The fusion food concept can elicit an eye roll from more jaded foodies,
but Subculture pulls off something that a lot of other restaurants can't:
true ingenuity with none of the pretension. Hidden away in a strip mall,
this little restaurant combines South American, Asian, and Southern
flavors into unique dishes: pimento cheese empanadas, butternut
tacos, and, most triumphantly, an amazing hot chicken ramen.

JOSEPHINE

Map 4; 2316 12th Avenue South, 12 South; ///vision.metro.caller;
www.josephineon12th.com

The elegant brick facade sets the tone for dinner at Josephine.
Enveloped in an interior of darks woods and leather, this is where
Nashvillians head when they want to show how grown up they are.

Parents in town? In-laws visiting? A promotion to celebrate? The above would all work nicely here. And the food – American farmhouse cuisine with a distinctly Southern twist – is set to impress.

>> Don't leave without trying the shaved beef tongue starter. It's deliciously decadent, and you can mark it off your foodie bucket list.

HENRIETTA RED

Map 2; 1200 4th Avenue North, Germantown; ///tamed.unions.bulb; www.henriettared.com

You know you're in a great restaurant when the decor is just as lovely as the food. Henrietta Red's bright and minimalist space is punctuated with cool mid-century furniture, making this a gorgeous place for date night. As for the food and drink, chef Julia Sullivan and sommelier Allie Poindexter are all about pairing fresh seafood with good wine. Set the mood with a bottle of chardonnay, or perhaps even champagne, before sharing a platter of oysters. It'll be a night to remember.

HUSK

Map 1; 37 Rutledge Street, Rutledge Hill; ///played.play.cycles; www.husknashville.com

Step inside Husk and you'll first see a giant chalkboard announcing exactly where the ingredients for tonight's menu have come from. You'll also note that everything listed is local, seasonal, and fresh. This is exactly what Husk is all about: celebrating the flavors of the South, like okra, sassafras, and country ham. Don't be afraid to get dolled up, by the way – this is where locals dine when they're feeling fancy.

Cheap Eats

There are times when you just want something cheap and cheerful and, thankfully, Nashville has a wealth of spots that plate up good, simple food. You don't need to dress up or have a reservation – just come hungry.

GABBY'S BURGERS

Map 4; 493 Humphreys Street, Wedgewood-Houston;
///couple.open.train; www.gabbysburgersandfries.com

Sometimes you don't want your burger to be pretty. You want it to be an indulgent, sloppy masterpiece with buttery grilled buns and all the accoutrements. And that's where Gabby's comes in. This casual spot,

Shh!

You know you've found a diamond in the rough when it doesn't even have a website. Mini Mart *(1600 Foster Avenue)* is part-deli, part-*carnicería*, where you can pick up mouthwatering breakfast tacos, fresh ceviche, and chorizo for your next cookout. The space feels like a Brooklyn bodega and only has room for a few people standing in line, making this a great spot to grab a cheap bite to go.

 Gabby's is a lunch-only joint and closes very promptly at 2:30pm every day, so get there early.

popular with 9-to-5ers on their lunch break, has perfected patties made from grass-fed beef. Pair with sweet potato fries and a milkshake for the complete experience.

SLIM & HUSKY'S PIZZA BEERIA

Map 2; 911 Buchanan Street, North Nashville; //stale.bravo.shins; www.slimandhuskys.com

Run by three Tennessee State University grads, this artisan pizzeria specializes in build-your-own pizzas using locally sourced ingredients. The space is full of personality thanks to the murals inspired by Spike Lee's *School Daze* and lyrics from "Tennessee" by hip-hop group Arrested Development. The owners keep community at the heart of the business by providing employment opportunities and hosting events. More good news: a second location can be found Downtown, making it the first Black-owned business on Broadway.

» Don't leave without checking out the events calendar – expect DJs, cocktails, games, and (of course) great food.

CONEHEADS

Map 3; 1315 Dickerson Pike, East Nashville; ///risk.curl.factories; www.coneheadscw.com/eat

Fried chicken, shrimp, and cauliflower are served in waffle cones at this East Nashville outpost, which takes its inspiration from 90s movie *Coneheads* (and the *SNL* sketch of the same name). Hungry beyond reason? Add a topper of the "best damn grits" or mac 'n' cheese.

Liked by the locals

"I have the best customers in the world – they all come in and say that it feels like grandma's house. You can have a state representative sitting next to a construction worker, sitting next to a stay-at-home mom, who all just needed to get out and have some lunch. And everyone's having a conversation."

ALPHONSO ANDERSON,
OWNER OF BIG AL'S DELI

BIG AL'S DELI

**Map 2; 1828 4th Avenue North, Germantown; ///defend.leaps.drips;
www.bigalsdeliandcatering.com**

You just know when a place has heart. Take Big Al's Deli, an itty-bitty spot that serves homestyle Southern noms. Arrive early to score one of the 16 seats and tuck into $2 biscuits (and gravy, obviously) or one of the filling entrées. Whatever you order, it'll feel like a hug from Big Al.

» Don't leave without ordering the legendary herb-roasted chicken. It's good enough to make you weep.

RED HEADED STRANGER

**Map 3; 305 Arrington Street, East Nashville; ///start.pinks.look;
www.redheadedstrangertacos.com**

On a quiet, residential street, a large neon sign directs the hungry to Red Headed Stranger. Inside, beanie-wearing hipsters chow down on the yummiest, gooiest Tex-Mex tacos this side of Austin (they even come wrapped in foil, like they're supposed to). Fun flavors like whipped feta and tater tot tacos are the queso on top of this local favorite.

MITCHELL DELICATESSEN

**Map 3; 1306 McGavock Pike, East Nashville; ///spice.bells.unions;
www.mitchelldeli.com**

It's all about the humble sandwich at this local stalwart, where meats are cured and smoked in-house (veggies and vegans, don't you worry: there are options for you, too). Copy the locals by ordering the house classic: the turkey avocado. You won't regret it.

Global Grub

Nashville might be a "big small town" but, goodness gracious, is it multicultural. And the food scene echoes this rich diversity – we're talking Caribbean, Kurdish, Mexican, and Mediterranean (to name a few cuisines).

MERENGUE CAFE

Map 4; 654 West Iris Drive, Berry Hill; ///names.flags.pace; www.merengue-cafe.business.site

This Berry Hill spot beckons with the aromas of spiced meats, garlic and other Caribbean goodies. Come hungry: you'll want to order the so-tender-you-could-cry stewed chicken and the garlicky *mofongo*. Wash everything down with a big, refreshing glass of passion fruit juice out on the patio. Just the ticket.

EPICE

Map 4; 2902 12th Avenue South, 12 South; ///fault.harsh.driver; www.epicenashville.com

Epice's sleek, modern space is a blank canvas for the vibrant food it plates up. Foodies love the family-owned place for its unfailingly friendly staff and stunningly presented Lebanese plates. We're talking dishes like lahmeh, a divine pistachio-crusted rack of lamb and sayadeya, a delicate grilled fish. Pair these flavors with an exquisite craft cocktail like the Saz "Arak," a twist on the classic rye cocktail featuring *arak*, a spirit made from grapes and anise.

THE SMILING ELEPHANT

Map 4; 2213 8th Avenue South, Melrose; ///trying.solid.scuba; www.thesmilingelephant.com

Ask any Nashvillian where to find the best Thai food and they'll send you here. Smiling Elephant makes arguably the best pad thai in the city (no overly sweet sauce to be found) and gorgeously rich and creamy curries. Oh, and fans of gluten-free, rejoice: Smiling Elephant has numerous tasty dishes for you, too.

HOUSE OF KABOB

Map 4; 407 West Thompson Lane, South Nashville; ///gentle.buzz.linen; (615) 333-3711

Did you know that Nashville is home to the largest Kurdish community in the entire US? Hamid Hasan and his family arrived in Nashville in 1993, part of a wave of Kurdish refugees that formed the backbone of a community now 15,000 strong. After working in the kitchen of a Persian restaurant in high school, Hasan became the owner and manager – and remaned it House of Kabob – at just 19. Today his restaurant showcases authentic Kurdish fare, such as the ever popular and flavorful skewers of chicken, salmon, and lamb.

» Don't leave without sampling the ice cream, made with rosewater and saffron, and topped with pistachios.

GREKO GREEK STREET FOOD

Map 3; 704 Main Street, East Nashville; ///deeply.frozen.social;
www.grekostreetfood.com

The family behind this restaurant have worked hard to transplant
diners from East Nashville to Athens. How? With authentic street
food (based on their beloved grandma Yia-Yia's recipes) and a
Greek hip-hop soundtrack. The result? A cool, no-frills hangout.

ROSEPEPPER CANTINA

Map 3; 1907 Eastland Avenue, East Nashville; ///feeds.gallons.grant:
www.rosepepper.com

This is the kind of Mexican that everyone wants at the end of their
street, where every day of the year feels like Cinco de Mayo. Pals
stroll down to Rosepepper for their weekday taco fix before locals
from other parts of the city travel across the river for a weekend
feast of fajitas and margaritas on the festively decorated patio.

» Don't leave without getting a photo in front of the restaurant's
famous sign, where a new and hilarious message (like "Abs are great
but have you tried tacos?") appears daily.

RIDDIM N SPICE

Map 2; 2116 Meharry Boulevard, North Nashville; ///calls.exile.trips;
www.riddimnspice.com

Once a food truck, now a plant-filled brick-and-mortar, Riddim N
Spice brings the combined rhythms and spices of Jamaica, Cuba,
Haiti, and Puerto Rico to Music City. Chef Kamal Kalokoh has cooked

for the likes of Drake and Rhianna but, these days, he's whipping up plates of jerk chicken (with heat levels from mild to "fiyah"), bowls of cucumber mango salad, and pans of rum cake for the good people of North Nashville. All to the irresistibly catchy beats of reggaeton.

CHAUHAN ALE & MASALA HOUSE
Map 2; 123 12th Avenue North, The Gulch; ///serves.fees.rams;
www.chauhannashville.com

Indian spices make their way into everything (seriously, *everything*) at Chauhan Ale & Masala House – even the whiskey sours. With her starters, chef Maneet Chauhan celebrates both her Indian heritage and affection for the South with Indian takes on Tennessee classics (think hot chicken pakoras). Mains, on the other hand, are more about traditional, rich curries. Enjoy all of this with a backdrop of Bollywood movies projected onto the restaurant walls.

Shh!

Tucked away in Woodbine, Pupusería Reina La Bendición *(3003 Nolensville Pike)* flies under the radar. This little Salvadoran restaurant is a joyous place: rows of paper lanterns and flags hang from the ceiling, colorful juices bubble enticingly behind the counter, and families chow down on comforting bowls of grub. Order your *pupusas* (thick corn cakes) stuffed with beans, cheese, *chicharrón* (pork skin), or *loroco* (edible flowers native to El Salvador).

Built in 1906 by German immigrant Henry Neuhoff, the **Neuhoff Meat-Packing Plant** is being redeveloped to house local businesses.

3RD AVENUE NORTH

4TH AVENUE NORTH

5TH AVENUE NORTH

MONROE STREET

Stop for pizza at CITY HOUSE

Refuel with a pizza at cozy City House, where Italian dishes are given a Southern twist.

4

GERMANTOWN

MADISON STREET

5

Time for tea from STEAM BOYS

Grab a boba tea to go and stop for a while to drink in the views of the Cumberland River.

1

3

Snag a treat at THE CUPCAKE COLLECTION

This family-run bakery makes everything from scratch. Pop in to buy a cupcake for later.

Fuel up at RED BICYCLE

Start the day with a sweet or savory crepe from this cute sidewalk café, and tuck in under the shade of a neighborhood tree.

6

Indulge at GEIST

Once a forge run by German immigrant John Geist, this spot is now an uber-chic restaurant. Gorge on upscale fare, like filet mignon, and enjoy decadent cocktails.

STREET

JEFFERSON

ROSA L PARKS BOULEVARD

7TH AVENUE NORTH

6TH AVENUE NORTH

3RD AVENUE NORTH

Stroll through NASHVILLE FARMERS' MARKET

2

Meet local farmers, pick up some fresh produce, and find inspiration for how to use it at a seasonal cooking class.

Since 1980, Germantown has honored its roots by celebrating Oktoberfest in **Bicentennial Park**, complete with beers and bratwurst.

| 0 meters | 300 |
| 0 yards | 300 |

DOWNTOWN

A day sampling food
in Germantown

The comforting smells of good cooking have lingered in the streets of Germantown since the late 1800s, when European immigrants settled here. Fast-forward to today, and the area abounds with foodie spots. If you want to taste Nashville in all its super-local inventiveness, Germantown will give you a taste in a few blocks.

1. Red Bicycle
1200 5th Avenue
North, Suite 104; www.
redbicyclecoffee.com
///bound.monks.verge

**2. Nashville
Farmers' Market**
900 Rosa L. Parks
Boulevard; www.nashville
farmersmarket.org
///purple.trash.paid

3. The Cupcake Collection
1213 6th Avenue North; www.
thecupcakecollection.com
///liner.leap.crown

4. City House
1222 4th Avenue North;
www.cityhousenashville.com
///warm.bonus.flank

5. Steam Boys
1200 2nd Avenue North;
www.steamboys.com
///found.shield.limbs

6. Geist
311 Jefferson Street;
www.geistnashville.com
///force.leave.curry

Bicentennial Park ///sank.activism.circle

Neuhoff Meat-Packing Plant ///tiger.vocab.badly

EAST
NASHVILLE

Jefferson
Street
Bridge

Cumberland River

DRINK

When locals aren't tapping their feet at a concert they're chatting to their neighbors in a coffee shop, kicking back in a craft brewery, or drinking in the view from a rooftop bar.

Breweries and Distilleries

First came breweries, then whiskey distilleries, and now a booming craft beer movement – Nashville has long loved its breweries and distilleries, and there are a surprising number for a city of this size.

BEARDED IRIS BREWING

Map 2; 101 Van Buren Street, Germantown; ///jungle.fees.guilty; www.beardedirisbrewing.com

Bearded Iris is a refreshing take on the usual industrial-feeling taproom (think fancy vintage furniture, chandeliers, and pool tables). At the long, regal bar, beer lovers gather to swap stories, make plans to take over the world, and, most importantly, sample the brewery's hazy IPAs.

JACKALOPE

Map 4; 429B Houston Street, Wedgewood-Houston; ///visit.among.float; www.jackalopebrew.com

The general vibe at this women-owned brewery is Wes Anderson-meets-the-desert, thanks to the bright splashes of color and huge cacti. Affectionately called "The Ranch," the taproom pulls some of

 Jackalope regularly hosts events, like free yoga, in the brewery. Check social media to see what's coming up.

Nashville's most recognizable names: the Thunder Ann IPA and Bear Walker Maple Brown Ale are both city staples, and best tried on their home turf.

NELSON'S GREEN BRIER DISTILLERY

Map 2; 1414 Clinton Street, The Gulch; ///prep.remove.inches; www.greenbrierdistillery.com

During the Civil War, a German immigrant called Charles Nelson introduced the world to a new product – Tennessee whiskey. Filtered through charcoal and aged in oak barrels, the drink was an immediate hit but, sadly, Prohibition shut production down. That was until one fateful day in 2006, when two young descendants stumbled on a preserved bottle of his whiskey and decided to continue in the family spirit. The result? This welcoming distillery in the Gulch.

» **Don't leave without** joining a distillery tour and buying a bottle of Louisa's liqueur (named after Nelson's pioneering wife).

SOUTHERN GRIST

Map 3; 1201 Porter Road, East Nashville; ///jumps.puzzle.petty; www.southerngristbrewing.com

It's all about experimental beers at this spunky brewery. Southern Grist churns out fun creations like Fluffernutter stouts but it really flexes its talent when it comes to sours, which come in playful flavors like boysenberry and blueberry cobbler. Don't miss the silky beers brewed with lactose – inspired stuff.

Solo, Pair, Crowd

Order a pint for you, beers for two, or a round for the crew at these unique Nashville breweries.

FLYING SOLO
Brews of every kind

When you can't decide if you're in the mood for beer or coffee, head to Living Waters Brewing where you can sip on either while reading the stories behind each brew.

IN A PAIR
Let the spirit lead

Inspired by Martin Luther (who, believe it or not, had a brewery), Black Abbey creates Belgian-style ales that are served up in its cathedral-like fellowship hall. Take a tour before catching up over an inspired pint.

FOR A CROWD
Patio hangs for all

With a huge beer garden and patio, there's no better place to meet friends for darts, drinks, and hangs than East Nashville Beer Works. Furry friends are also welcome.

CORSAIR DISTILLERY

Map 2; 1200 Clinton Street #110, Marathon Village; ///darker.voice.audit;
www.corsairdistillery.com

Welcome to what was the first legal craft distillery in Nashville post-Prohibition. Take a seat in the distillery's taproom and sample Corsair's fruity malt whiskeys or enjoy a craft gin-based cocktail. If you're lucky, the intrepid distillery cat (called Pizza) might pop by for a cuddle.

TENNESSEE BREW WORKS

Map 1; 809 Ewing Avenue, Downtown; ///output.served.acid;
www.tnbrew.com

After a hard day's work, locals have one place in mind: the double-decker patio of this crowd-pleasing brewery. Traditionalists clutch draft regulars, like the State Park American Blonde Ale, while the curious prefer to sip seasonal brews, like the Wildwood Flower Honey Blonde Ale. Join them on a Wednesday when bluegrass bands perform.

» Don't leave without soaking up the booze via a Southern grilled cheese – a combo of white cheddar, goat cheese, and apple butter.

NASHVILLE CRAFT DISTILLERY

Map 4; 514 Hagan Street, Wedgewood-Houston; ///scouts.lows.total;
www.nashvillecraft.com

This small-but-mighty distillery creates locally inspired spirits; we're talking whiskey, gin, absinthe, and liqueurs. Even the bottle labels are so Nashville, with designs inspired by Hatch Show Print (p89). Take a tour to discover how the passionate team source and use local flavors.

Cocktail Joints

Nashville may have a beer-and-whiskey reputation, but its cocktail scene rivals cities double its size. Bartenders stir things up with some seriously creative concoctions, including genuinely delicious mocktails.

FOX BAR & COCKTAIL CLUB

Map 3; 2905B Gallatin Pike, East Nashville; ///closer.edits.emerge; www.thefoxnashville.com

Oh, the luxury of this place. Sumptuous velvet booths, moody lighting, and Art Deco finishings mean you'll be adjusting your imaginary fur shawl and speaking in 20s slang the minute you're seated. As for the cocktails, they're works of art, served in the most gorgeous glassware. Happily, equal attention is paid to the mocktails – the seedlip-based Paper Moon is truly celestial.

WILLIE B'S

Map 2; 918 Buchanan Street, North Nashville; ///posts.asserts.blasts; www.thewilliebs.com

With its greenery, modern lighting, and slick marble tabletops, this stylish lounge-turned-restaurant is fashionable, y'all. Come dressed to the nines to enjoy live music and DJ sets while sipping on one of the creative cocktails or a frozen daiquiri. Owner Christopher Jones named the place for his grandmother, who taught him to cook, and his drinks menu keeps community in mind, denoting which cocktails are made with Black-owned spirits. If you're hungry, Willie B's New Orleans-inflected food is the real deal.

BASTION

Map 4; 434 Houston Street, Suite 110, Wedgewood-Houston;
///stacks.class.voter; www.bastionnashville.com

Bastion doesn't take itself too seriously, with nostalgic arcade games, quirky wall art, and epic "tables" built into the back wall that resemble an adult jungle gym. Tempted by the chilled digs and sunny cocktail menu, young professionals flock here en masse to blow off steam. As for those living that booze-free life? Lucky for them, Bastion's mocktails are some of the best in the city.

» Don't leave without trying your hand at the ring-toss game after a cocktail (or two). Before you know it, you'll have a whole crowd cheering you on.

Try it!
MIXOLOGY MASTERCLASS

If you fancy honing your mixology skills, head to Downtown's Liquor Lab (www. liquorlab.com). Under the tutelage of experts, you'll learn the history of various cocktails and how to craft that perfect sip.

PATTERSON HOUSE

Map 5; 1711 Division Street, Midtown; ///green.summer.tilt;
www.thepattersonnashville.com

Nashville's original speakeasy (there can be a lengthy wait: you've been warned) serves up exquisite Prohibition-era cocktails that perfectly echo the gorgeous vintage decor. Though the vibe is distinctly old-timey, the strict house rules are refreshingly modern: no cell phones, no drinks without a seat, and no hitting on strangers.

OLD GLORY

Map 4; 1200 Villa Place, Suite 103, Edgehill; ///worth.lonely.awards;
www.oldglorynashville.com

The entrance to Old Glory is marked by a large gold triangle, an understated portal into one of Nashville's most unique cocktail bars. Cross the threshold and you'll find a huge hidden space – an old,

When the green lantern comes on at Tempered Fine Chocolates in Germantown, it means the daytime chocolate shop has turned into The Green Hour, a secret absinthe bar *(www. greenhournashville.com)*. Choose from dozens of different absinthes (who knew there were so many?) and sweeten your spirit by using an old-school dripper to strain water through a sugar cube. Better yet, each drink comes with a bite of homemade chocolate for a chaser.

underground laundromat, actually – with vaulted ceilings and a cool, rock-hewn bar. Here, Nashville's trendiest gather to order creative cocktails like Two Suns, a medicinal blend of gin, turmeric tea, honey, and lemon. Stay late for DJs, drag queens, and acrobats.

ATTABOY

Map 3; 8 Mcferrin Avenue, East Nashville; ///brace.slang.change; www.attaboy.us

The small white building housing Attaboy might seem austere but don't let that fool you. Knock on the door to enter, and you'll be guided into a dark, intimate bar where you just might taste the best cocktail you've ever had. That's not an overstatement – Attaboy's sister, in NYC, frequents the World's 50 Best Bars list, and the two are inextricably linked in style and quality. The best bit? Attaboy has no menu. Tell the bartender your tastes and they'll create a drink just for you.

PEARL DIVER

Map 3; 1008 Gallatin Avenue, East Nashville; ///sudden.fades.into; www.pearldivernashville.com

Things we love about tiki bars: perfect mai tais and the feeling of escape right in our backyard. Things we don't love: kitsch, overly-sweet cocktails. Fortunately, there's nothing but things to love at Pearl Diver. Meet hip locals sipping well-balanced cocktails and – when it's particularly hot out – have a lie down on one of the retro cabanas.

>> **Don't leave without** ordering a "yum yum" – a punchy mix of dark rum, house-made coconut cream, and lemongrass.

Rooftop Bars

While Nashville's Downtown is modest in size, it has enough towers to foster a creative rooftop scene. These high-flying bars offer urban explorers the perfect place to kick back and enjoy some of those Southern rays.

L27 ROOFTOP LOUNGE

Map 1; 807 Clark Place, Downtown; ///forced.rope.puzzle; www.l27nashville.com

Get ready to channel your inner influencer because L27 is one of the most photogenic rooftops in Nashville. Loungers, daybeds, and cabanas sit in an attentive ring around the deck's centerpiece – a gorgeous infinity pool that seems to spill down the 26 floors below. This is the place to catch that fiery Tennessean sunset, ideally with a glass of Sky Rye (whiskey, sage, lemon juice, cardamom, and orange bitters).

RARE BIRD

Map 1; 200 4th Avenue North, Top Floor, Downtown; ///risk.works.calm; www.rarebirdrooftop.com

Yes, the Art Deco lobby of old-bank-turned-hotel Noelle is deliciously retro-cool, but keep on moving and get yourself to the 13th floor. Here you'll find Rare Bird, and the best views of Nashville's

Journey down to Noelle's hidden subtrarananean bar, which regularly hosts eccentric bar pop-ups. most iconic building: the AT&T tower, lovingly referred to by locals as the Batman Building. Pair the scenery with a glass of wine and you're onto a winner.

L.A. JACKSON

Map 1; 401 11th Avenue South, The Gulch; ///object.chew.loud; www.lajacksonbar.com

The vibe is *"Mad Men* go on vacation" at this stylish rooftop bar, where well-dressed friends and businessmen loosening their ties come to see and be seen. Atop the classy Thompson Hotel, the patio has unmatched views across Downtown – the perfect backdrop for sipping creative cocktails (called punny things like Tequillin' Me Softly and Sunday Scaries). And, when a typically Southern thundershower makes an appearance, the gorgeous indoor bar is on hand for shelter.

WHITE LIMOZEEN

Map 5; 101 20th Avenue North, West End; ///vivid.drop.dating; www.graduatehotels.com

There's one thing Nashvillians agree on: Dolly Parton for president. And if we can't have that, second best is a Dolly themed rooftop bar (and restaurant), which White Limozeen delivers with pizzazz. Fringed umbrellas and jolly pink seats pepper the patio, which is particularly popular with girlfriends meeting after working nine to five (ahem).

» Don't leave without tucking into some seafood while you're here. The marinated mussels and salmon sashimi are particularly good.

Liked by the locals

"There's something about sipping a drink on a rooftop with city views that makes you feel like a million bucks. And in Nashville, it's no different. Our rooftop bars all share creative cocktails, tasty bites, bangin' music, and epic views. Find me at one of these rooftops all summer long, soaking up the sun!"

PAIGE MUIRHEAD,
WEALTH MANAGEMENT ASSOCIATE

ACME FEED & SEED

Map 1; 101 Broadway, Downtown; ///fetch.begun.risen;
www.acmefeedandseed.com

Okay, it's just four stories above street level but we couldn't miss this one. Housed in an old farm supply building that used to host country music jamborees, Acme is all about the music. Down-to-earth locals journey to the modern day honky-tonk to watch new artists perform, sip boozy slushees, and chow down on Southern fare.

>> **Don't leave without** getting the details of Acme's radio show, which offers a launchpad for young musicians (like the Opry once did).

GEORGE JONES

Map 1; 128 2nd Avenue North, Downtown; ///voice.races.latest;
www.georgejones.com

A Nashville bar named after a country star is a cliché, but we don't plan to stop loving this one anytime soon. After exploring the George Jones Museum, head to the rooftop for gorgeous views over the Cumberland River – lovely for watching the boats go by, drink in hand.

BOBBY HOTEL

Map 1; 230 4th Avenue North, Downtown; ///prom.funded.veal;
www.bobbyhotel.com

Picture this: checkerboard tiles in 70s shades, a vintage bus decked out with bar seats, young locals hanging out in jaunty cabanas; everything about this rooftop lounge feels like a throwback. Haven't listened to live music in a couple of hours? Don't worry, there's a live stage here, too.

Patio Bars

*Patio-sittin' is a weekend pastime in Nashville.
Front porches are essential in the South – what
with the many months of warm weather – and the
city's bars give the people what they need.*

12 SOUTH TAPROOM

**Map 4; 2318 12th Avenue South, 12 South; ///hunt.pools.spends;
www.12southtaproom.com**

On a balmy day, this is the place to be. The close-knit community
of 12 South congregate here to chitchat, clink craft beers, take part
in trivia nights, and generally bask in the sunshine. And if it starts
raining cats and dogs (seriously: when it rains, it pours), the patio is
covered so you won't have to scramble for shelter for you and your
precious pint. Happy days.

VON ELROD'S BEER HALL

**Map 2; 1004 4th Avenue North, Germantown; ///care.bills.land;
www.vonelrods.com**

A modern German beer hall isn't what you'd expect to find a stone's
throw from Downtown Nashville but, boy, it's a welcome discovery.
Paying homage to the area's German roots, Von Elrod's has a

Catch a game at nearby First Horizon Park, home of the city's minor league baseball, after a drink here.

whopping 36 beer taps. Head to the patio where it's buzzier and saddle up on one of the long communal benches, where you'll make friends with your neighbor in no time.

NEVER NEVER

Map 4; 413 Houston Street, Wedgewood-Houston;
///chimp.senses.asleep; www.nevernevernashville.com

Hidden away in Wedgewood-Houston, Never Never sits small and humble in an old welding shop. Inside, the space is moody (a neon sign reading "Time will tell, we won't" upping the intrigue), while outside two patios are peppered with vintage lawn furniture and picnic tables, making it perfect for a slightly-more-than-casual date. No bells or whistles, just a cute, down-to-earth spot that's rightly loved by locals.

SANDBAR

Map 5; 3 City Avenue #500, Sylvan Park; ///bought.gender.nurses;
www.sandbarnashville.com

Good news for current and former spring-breakers: this fun-loving patio bar does its best to bring the sun and sand to Music City. Hours are whiled away here sipping super-fresh juice (topped up with liquor) from carved-out coconuts and pineapples, and watching the local volleyball league play a game or two on the bar's courts. Blink and you're practically in Florida.

» Don't leave without ordering one of the non-alcoholic drinks served in a Capri Sun-like bag for pure thirst-quenching refreshment.

M.L. ROSE

**Map 4; 2535 8th Avenue South, Suite 107, Melrose;
///intent.cheese.natively; www.melrose.com**

You'd never know that this nondescript burger joint has the area's best selection of craft beers and the loveliest patio. Make your way through the football-watching crowds clamoring at the bar and out back where you'll find an ivy-covered yard dotted with picnic benches and strung with lights. It's the neighborhood's prime spot for a seasonal brew.

BLUE MOON WATERFRONT GRILLE

**Map 6; 525 Basswood Drive, The Nations; ///ozone.paints.darker;
www.bluemoongrille.com**

Hankering for a drink with a view? Enter Blue Moon. This floating waterfront restaurant transports patrons to New England, with its idyllic outlook over the river. Watch boats bobbing on the water as you sip a crisp white Zinfandel – the ideal end to a long ol' week.

DISKIN CIDER

**Map 4; 1235 Martin Street, Wedgewood-Houston; ///herb.spare.hook;
www.diskincider.com**

Beer may be king around these parts, but Nashville's first cidery is changing all that. Exciting takes on the apple-based tipple keep a steady stream of thirsty guests coming through the doors. Diskin's indoor space is smart and airy but the real draw is the large side patio. Outfitted with low-slung benches and fire pits, the space is particularly buzzy on the first Saturday of the month, when those on the Wedgewood-Houston art crawl end up here to lounge, sip satisfying ciders, and talk all things art.

» **Don't leave without** trying the Six One Five, a fruity tea cider designed to evoke memories of front porches, lakes, and fireflies.

PHARMACY BURGER PARLOR AND BEER GARDEN

Map 3; 731 Mcferrin Avenue, East Nashville; ///waters.slap.forced; www.thepharmacyburger.com

Aside from the fact that this place serves incredible burgers (we're talking the most succulent patties, made with Tennessee-raised beef) and astonishingly good house-made sausages, here you'll find an utterly charming beer garden. Lush foliage draped with fairy lights creates a leafy backdrop for laid-back 30-somethings, families, and out-of-towners. There's also an impressive range of house-made sodas, shakes, and malts – perfect for a day sat in the sunshine.

URBAN COWBOY

Map 3; 1603 Woodland Street, East Nashville; ///swear.lion.rugs; www.urbancowboy.com

Outdoor fire pits and Southwestern-style touches will have you curling up under an alpaca blanket and staring at the stars at Urban Cowboy. Tucked behind an adorable bed and breakfast of the same name, the patio is popular with hipsters in chambray shirts and wide-brim hats, who sit by the fire and share stories of adventures on the road.

Cozy Bars

What's at the heart of Nashville's coziest bars? The people – you won't find a more inclusive or friendly bunch. Stop by to sink into a sofa, chat to the regulars, and feel at home away from home.

THE CENTENNIAL

Map 5; 5115 Centennial Boulevard, The Nations; ///dark.transit.hung; www.centennialnashville.com

Just want to watch the game somewhere comfy, a craft beer in hand? This laid-back bar, where no one ever dresses up (and where a strangely compelling amount of Patrick Swayze-themed art covers the walls), is just the ticket. Bonus points for having the friendliest staff in the neighborhood.

ALLEY TAPS

Map 1; 162 Printers Alley, Downtown; ///friend.economies.rice; www.alleytapsnashville.com

On the less trafficked side of Printers Alley, Alley Taps hangs tight to Nashville's singer-songwriter tradition with a nightly schedule of talent playing original tunes. The place feels intimate and undiscovered, thanks largely to its underground, rock-hewn locale.

 Come with some small bills for the performers' tip jars – it's part of the live music culture.

Draw up a chair alongside those in-the-know to enjoy a performance (of jazz, if you time your visit right), whiskey in hand.

SANTA'S PUB

Map 4; 2225 Bransford Avenue, Berry Hill;
///paid.serve.escape; (615) 593-1872

One surreal night singing karaoke at Santa-themed Santa's Pub will leave you questioning if the place is real or if it was a fever dream. This beer-only, cash-only, somewhat-smoky-but-eternally-festive dive bar is a true local icon, attracting students, old-timers, and all the gang with its year-round holiday decorations and St Nick lookalike owner, Elmer Denzel "Santa" Irwin. Don your most kitschy sweaters and prepare to belt out some iconic 80s power ballads – here, it really is Christmas every day.

BAR SOVEREIGN

Map 1; 514 Rep. John Lewis Way South, Downtown;
///fired.hungry.mash; www.barsovereign.com

Vaguely nautical, vaguely tropical, vaguely speakeasy, Bar Sovereign defies categorization and likewise pulls a varied crowd. Grab a seat at the bar or, when it's cooler, relax next to the fireplace while you enjoy one of the bartender's beautiful cocktails (or mocktails).

≫ Don't leave without getting a steaming bowl of ramen, the perfect comfort food from Black Dynasty, served out back.

Solo, Pair, Crowd

No matter where you are in town, or who you're with, you're never far from a Nashville bar to get snug in.

FLYING SOLO
Get comfy in a jazzy café

Americano Lounge in Wedgewood-Houston is the perfect spot for a rainy day date with yourself. Sink down in a velvet chair, tune into the music, and pick your poison – coffee or cocktail?

IN A PAIR
A swanky night for two

In a stone-walled basement on Printers Alley, Skull's Rainbow Room is the ideal spot to cuddle up with a couple of cocktails. Expect dim lighting, live jazz, and burlesque performances.

FOR A CROWD
Old-fashioned fun

Earnest Bar & Hideaway is like a cozy old library that Mr. Hemingway would approve of. Gather with your friends in the decadent (but spacious) Wedgewood-Houston bar and clink decorative cocktail coupes.

GREENHOUSE BAR

Map 5; 2211 Bandywood Drive, Green Hills; ///lush.ripe.boat; (615) 385-3357

On a drizzly day in Nashville, there are few places more inviting than this little rustic haven. Inside the greenhouse, tables and chairs sit higgledy-piggledy on gravel, and thriving, cacti, succulents, and ferns cover every inch of spare space. Add the pitter-patter of rain on the roof and you'll find yourself hunkering down for a second tipsy tea.

» Don't leave without ordering a mojito, made with mint freshly picked from the greenhouse garden.

DUKE'S

Map 3; 1000 Main Street, East Nashville; ///direct.soaks.test; www.dukesbarnashville.com

Duke's is one of those bars that you don't have to overthink; everyone rocks jeans and t-shirts (and still looks cool doing it), and drink options are scrawled in sharpie on the wall behind the bar. Regulars are at the heart of this local dive – they even have drinks named after them.

WALDEN

Map 3; 2909 Gallatin Pike B, East Nashville; ///career.economies.kings; www.waldenbar.com

Inspired by the woods made famous by writer Henry David Thoreau, Walden is all about the simple life. Under the bar's low, wood-beamed ceiling, laid-back locals lounge on benches piled with pillows, sip Moscow mules, and shoot the breeze with their loved ones.

Coffee Shops

Creatives and coffee go hand-in-hand, so it follows that an artistic city like Nashville has a wealth of coffee shops. Make like a local and head to one of these spots to get caffeinated with the community.

CREMA COFFEE

Map 1; 15 Hermitage Avenue, Downtown; ///loans.job.manage; www.crema-coffee.com

We love a conscious coffee shop so we naturally adore Crema, a carbon-neutral and zero-waste roaster in the heart of Nashville. The creation of husband and wife Ben and Rachel, Crema has won a number of awards for its kaleidoscope of bean flavors; step inside the cheerful Downtown outlet to carry out your own taste test.

Try it!
BECOME A BARISTA

Tired of your standard drip coffee but know nothing about brewing on your own? Learn how to bring out your coffee's best at one of Crema's hour-long coffee classes. Students also get discounts on coffee and gear.

RETROGRADE

**Map 3; 1305 Dickerson Pike, East Nashville; ///couple.wanted.famous;
www.retrogradecoffee.com**

This one's a great little place for a bit of downtime. Bypass the tables of
digital nomads, furiously typing at their laptops, en route to the
counter and order an inventive latte (butterscotch and cardamom,
you say?). If possible, get a seat by the storefront window – perfect for
watching the world go by, or starting that new paperback.

TEMPO

**Map 4; 2179 Nolensville Pike, South Nashville; ///fixed.soup.pure;
www.temponashville.com**

When Texan percussionist Javier Solis arrived in Nashville he set about
merging his affinity for quality coffee with Tex-Mex breakfast fare. The
result? The delightful Tempo. Javier and family remain at the helm of
this South Nashville outfit. And yes, of course there's a live music stage.
» Don't leave without pairing your morning coffee with a breakfast
taco. The chorizo and egg is especially hard to beat.

8TH & ROAST

**Map 5; 4104 Charlotte Avenue, West Nashville; ///shells.shout.valid;
www.8thandroast.com**

There are two things at the core of 8th & Roast: coffee and community.
Childhood chums Ed and Q ensure all their beans are ethically traded
and lovingly roast every one in-house. Swing by the West Nashville
store (the other is in Melrose) for a warm hello and hot espresso.

FROTHY MONKEY

Map 4; 2509 12th Avenue South, 12 South; ///fuel.serves.cards;
www.frothymonkey.com

On a tree-lined street in 12 South sits one of Nashville's most well-loved coffeehouses. Frothy Monkey is like a second home: stroller moms nurse rosemary honey lattes on the porch, groups gather after church for breakfast and a brew, and students discuss politics over cappuccinos. Even if you're just popping in for an Americano to-go, you'll feel part of the family.

FIDO

Map 5; 1812 21st Avenue South, Hillsboro Village; ///bake.output.violin;
www.bongojava.com

Fido is the place that locals take out-of-towners, and their dogs of course, when they want to show them the real Nashville. The decor is no frills and has a lovely lived-in feel, and the staff are reliably welcoming. But the top drawer? That's got to be the coffee – we're talking organic, fair trade, and full of seasonal flavors.

HUMPHREYS STREET COFFEE

Map 4; 424 Humphreys Street, Wedgewood-Houston;
///freed.darker.corn;www.humphreysstreet.com

We all had jobs as teens, but we're willing to bet you probably didn't work in a cool independent coffee shop that actually cared about your future. Humphreys Street Coffee is a nonprofit focused on supporting its community by employing and mentoring students of South Nashville. One hundred percent of their profits go towards programs and scholarships for their employees. Oh, and the coffee is seriously good, too.

» Don't leave without making like a millennial and ordering one of the creative avocado toasts. Toppings change with the seasons.

BARISTA PARLOR
Map 2; 1230 4th Avenue North, Germantown; ///loaf.hatch.newly;
www.baristaparlor.com

Beakers, high stools, and careful science. No, you're not back in chemistry class, but you are in a lab of sorts. Barista Parlor prides itself on experimenting to create the best brew, using different techniques to highlight the unique flavor of each roast. Watch the baristas, in leather aprons rather than lab coats, as they work the central coffee station like scientists perfecting a medicine (which, of course, coffee is).

Shh!

A lot of Nashville locals miss Headquarters, what with it being just 9 ft (3 m) wide *(www. hqsnashville.com)*. Look closely for the hanging, rusted metal sign that simply says "Coffee" and you've got to the entrance. Inside, the tiny space packs a lot of charm, with wooden beams, exposed brick walls, and posies of flowers dotted around. If you can find a spot to sit on the back deck, consider it your lucky day; if not, get your coffee to go and sip it while walking to Centennial Park *(p171)*.

An afternoon of
brewery hopping

Nashville has long taken its beer seriously. With the arrival of German immigrants in the 19th century came a love of beer, and breweries started popping up across the city. The most prominent was the Nashville Brewing Company, founded in 1859. Though the brewery no longer stands, its recipes have been passed down for generations, with many local brewers still using them today. Spend an afternoon exploring a new wave of craft brews, and raise a glass to Music City's hoppy legacy.

THE GULCH

I-40

I-65

1. Jackalope Brewing Company
429B Houston Street, Wedgewood-Houston; www.jackalopebrew.com ///visit.among.float

2. New Heights Brewing Company
928 Republican John Lewis Way South, Chestnut Hill; www. newheightsbrewing. com ///tribes.rated.cares

3. Tennessee Brew Works
809 Ewing Avenue, Downtown; www.tnbrew.com ///herbs.zips.lazy

4. Proper Saké Co.
628 Ewing Avenue, Downtown; www.proper sake.co ///grapes.league.legs

Rose Park

EDGEHILL

📍 **Diskin Cider** ///mutual.cheeks.union

Reservoir Park

KOREAN VETERANS BLVD

LAFAYETTE ST

RUTLEDGE
HILL

I-40

0 meters 400
0 yards 400

**End on a different note at
PROPER SAKÉ CO.**

Sample different styles of fresh, small
batch sake – all brewed by owner
Byron – right off the tap.

*A local historian has
used radar technology
to try to locate Nashville
Brewing Company's
abandoned beer cellars
under the city streets.*

4

6TH AVENUE SOUTH

EWING AVE

**Grab lunch at
TENNESSEE BREW
WORKS**

Sit out on the brewery's
huge patio and tuck into a
burger and craft beer,
made using ingredients
from Tennessee farms.

3

LAFAYETTE STREET

2ND AVENUE SOUTH

I-40

2

OAK ST

4TH AVENUE SOUTH

CHESTNUT
HILL

**Quaff a pint at
NEW HEIGHTS
BREWING COMPANY**

This no-frills craft microbrewery
is run by husband and wife Jeff
and Tracey. Order a pint and
enjoy with a dose of vitamin D
out in the lovely beer garden.

8TH AVENUE SOUTH

*Fort
Negley*

CHESTNUT ST

HOUSTON
STREET

1

*In 2012, **Diskin Cider**
opened as the city's only
craft cidery. The founders
learned under an English
cider master and only use
fresh-pressed apples.*

I-65

WEDGEWOOD-
HOUSTON

**Take a tour at
JACKALOPE
BREWING COMPANY**

It all started with a passion
for homebrewing and a
friendship formed in Scotland.
Join a tour to learn exactly
how the ladies of Jackalope
create their tasty beers.

SHOP

Nashvillians have been shopping small before it was cool, preferring homemade and secondhand over mass produced. And in a city of makers, who can blame them?

Home Touches

Nashvillians are stylish people and this doesn't stop at fashion. Locally made candles, colorful prints, and handwoven baskets make a house a home here. And you can buy a bit of Nashville to take home, too.

PADDYWAX CANDLE BAR

Map 4; 2934 Sidco Drive #140, Berry Hill; ///jets.miles.mock; www.thecandlebar.co

Remember when the gift of a candle was kind of disappointing? How times have changed. Drop into this gorgeous little shop to inhale row upon row of creatively scented soy candles, all hand-poured here in Nashville. Our favorites are from the author-inspired Library series, namely the Charlotte Brontë (rose geranium with

Try it!
WAXING LYRICAL

Prefer to make your own candle? Book a three-hour session for you and your squad at Paddywax's studio and create your own unique combination of wax and fragrance.

notes of nutmeg and sandalwood) and the Oscar Wilde (cedarwood, basil, and thyme). You'll leave the store with a bagful of deliciously scented presents for your friends (and, let's be honest, yourself).

HATCH SHOW PRINT

Map 1; 224 Rep. John Lewis Way South, Downtown; ///easy.pillow.loaf;
www.hatchshowprint.com

You'd struggle to find a local who doesn't have an artwork from Hatch Show Print adorning the walls of their house or apartment. The letterpress has been churning out striking advertisements since 1879, though it was in the mid-20th century that the family-run printmakers started making its iconic concert posters for the likes of Hank Williams and Louis Armstrong. Today the store continues to work closely with the Grand Ole Opry *(p118)* and the Ryman *(p116)*.

» Don't leave without joining a tour to get a closer look at Hatch Show's press stations and have a go at making a print yourself.

APPLE & OAK

Map 3; 717 Porter Road, East Nashville; ///firmly.influencing.desk;
www.appleandoaknash.com

Follow in the footsteps of design-forward Nashvillians and head to Apple & Oak. It was vintage Turkish rugs delivered via a weathered pickup truck that first put the store on the map. Along with its popular pre-loved rugs, the East Nashville outpost is packed with fun doormats (the "Hey Y'all" mat is especially hard to resist), colorful throws, and sexy vases, a lot of which are made by local artisans.

THE GOOD FILL

Map 3; 1106 Woodland Street, East Nashville;
///craft.snows.tree; www.thegoodfill.co

Eco-warriors are regulars at The Good Fill, placing treasures for
their bathrooms and kitchens in their overflowng baskets. It's all
thanks to hairstylist-turned-eco-advocate Megan Gill, who curates
sustainably made bath and kitchen products that either come in
reusable packaging or no packaging at all. This is a great stop if
you've got an empty shampoo bottle or you're after reusable
utensils, like stainless steel straws or bamboo toothbrushes.

OAK NASHVILLE

Map 5; 4200 Charlotte Avenue, Sylvan Park; ///narrow.issue.bossy;
www.oaknashville.com

When millennials want to show that they've got their lives together,
they go shopping in OAK Nashville. It's all about rural Southern style
at this home goods store (think basket planters, clay vases, and rustic
glassware). Better yet, the prices are mercifully wallet-friendly.

THE BOOKSHOP

Map 3; 1043 West Eastland Avenue, East Nashville;
///late.enhancement.soft; www.herbookshop.com

One of the few bookstores left in town, The Bookshop is a cozy nook
that specializes in beautifully designed coffee table books. The store
is curated by former book editor and all-round literary nut Joelle Herr,
who can often be seen tidying her beloved bookshelves. Flip through

While you're in the area visit Welcome Home, which has a great range of books and home goods.

photography and travel tomes, chat to Joelle, and buy something to spruce up your coffee table; it'll be the perfect read to go with your Sunday morning cup o' joe.

THISTLE FARMS

Map 5; 5122 Charlotte Avenue, West Nashville; ///likely.follow.under; www.thistlefarms.org

"Love Heals" is the motto at the heart of Thistle Farms and, boy, does this organization have heart. Its community of female employees – survivors of abuse, addiction, prostitution, and trafficking – create natural, small batch products for the home and body. Pop by for a chat with the ladies who work here and buy a candle, snuggly throw, or handcrafted basket to bring a little love into your own home. You'll likely spot Thistle Farms products in other shops around Nashville, too.

» Don't leave without enjoying a bit of self-care in Thistle Farms' café with a pot of tea and, more importantly, a slice of cake.

WHITE'S MERCANTILE

Map 4; 2908 12th Avenue South, 12 South; ///shots.scrap.audio; www.whitesmercantile.com

Old meets new at White's Mercantile, a general goods store based in an old gas filling station. Owned by singer-songwriter Holly Williams, the place is packed with home pieces that reflect her folksy style, like teak salad bowls and lemonade pitchers – ideal purchases to serve up lunch on the porch with your loved ones.

Southern Style

Music and fashion go hand-in-hand so it follows that this city has style. Not only that, Nashville has a wealth of sustainable brands and indie stores that'll make you feel like a star (even if you're just singing in the car).

ABEDNEGO

Map 2; 1212 4th Avenue North, Germantown; ///unit.factories.trails; www.abednegoboutique.com

When it comes to fashion, locals go wild for minimalist boho chic (take note: a wide-brimmed hat is a must) and ABEDNEGO is their one- stop-shop for such Music City style. Groups of chic girlfriends comb the store's rails and shelves, swooning over the frilled crop tops, floral skirts, and strappy sandals. Trust us when we say you'll likewise be seduced by the shop's floaty dresses and pairs of booties.

IMOGENE + WILLIE

Map 4; 2601 12th Avenue South, 12 South; ///angel.games.things; www.imogeneandwillie.com

A great pair of blue jeans is a staple in Nashville (many a country song has been written about them) and you can't do much better than Imogene + Willie, which uses premium denim hand-sewn here in the

US. Based in a retrofitted gas station, the store is part jeans shop, part community hub. It's not uncommon to see friends tossing a football in the parking lot and local artists strumming tunes in the courtyard.

VINNIE LOUISE

Map 4; 2308 12th Avenue South #2430, 12 South; ///cape.waddle.broke; www.vinnielouise.com

Style should be affordable, something that Vinnie Louise owner Ginny feels strongly about. Named for Ginny's stylish grandmother, the airy store is decked out with gingham dresses, denim rompers, and floral kimonos — all with wallet-friendly price tags. Not sure where to begin? The staff are some of the loveliest and on hand to help.

DRAPER JAMES

Map 4; 2608 12th Avenue South, 12 South; ///loans.wire.civil; www.draperjames.com

Football is kind of a big deal in the South. Locals love to tailgate — essentially get dolled up (smart shirts and cocktail dresses aren't uncommon), park up in the lot ahead of a game, and hang out with beers and snacks. And in Nashville they tailgate in real style, hitting up stores like Reese Witherspoon's stylish Draper James to get the right look. Here, guests are handed a glass of sweet tea as they peruse the rails of gingham sundresses and seersucker suits — perfect outfits for a truly Southern afternoon.

» Don't leave without taking the obligatory photo outside the blue-and-white candy-striped storefront.

ABLE

Map 5; 5022 Centennial Boulevard, The Nations; ///slower.frogs.clip; www.livefashionable.com

What started as an accessories line set up to create jobs for women exiting Ethiopia's sex industry is now a full fashion house that's all about empowering its female staff in Nashville and around the world. How? By paying them fairly and transparently. Browse ABLE's simple, stylish pieces that'll look just as good on a blogger as a boardroom boss.

» Don't leave without checking ABLE's events calendar for workshops, panel discussions about sustainable fashion, and warehouse sales.

BILLY REID

Map 4; 1200 Villa Place Unit 403, Wedgewood-Houston; ///rails.enjoy.trader; www.billyreid.com

Just south of Nashville is Muscle Shoals Sound Studio where Aretha Franklin and Wilson Pickett recorded tracks, and it's these soulful roots that inspire designer Billy Reid. His Nashville store feels like a moody man cave with its collection of beautiful shirts, suits, coats, and denim.

WHISKEY WATER

Map 3; 737 Porter Road, East Nashville; ///lunch.hops.vocab; www.shopwhiskeywater.com

The founder and editor of fashion blog The Whiskey Wolf opened this brick-and-mortar store to the delight of Nashville's rock 'n' rollers. Expect ripped jeans, leopard print dresses, and cool t-shirts that have things like "support your local dive bar" emblazoned across their front.

Liked by the locals

"The Nashville spirit is infectious. Stay here long enough and you're going to catch the creative bug. And don't let anyone tell you that it's limited to music. Nashville's maker community is thriving and is out to change the world one handcrafted product at a time."

CHRISTOPHER LESTER, FOUNDER OF CLIFTON + LEOPOLD, A NASHVILLE-BASED FASHION LINE

Foodie Gifts

Music might be the food of love but so is, well, food. Nashville is home to numerous artisanal makers who passionately craft foodie treats – the perfect gifts for your nearest and dearest.

GOO GOO CLUSTER

Map 1; 116 3rd Avenue South, Downtown; ///shed.behave.pack;

www.googoo.com

An indulgent dollop of marshmallow nougat, caramel, and peanuts all wrapped in a chocolate shell, the Goo Goo Cluster has been charming the masses since 1912. These candies are the perfect Nashville souvenir to take home for your friends (or your fridge). Don't stop at buying the candy as gifts; tuck into a Goo Goo themed ice cream sundae while you're here.

HONEYTREE MEADERY

Map 3; 918 Woodland Street, East Nashville; ///cried.brands.dozed;

www.honeytreemeadery.com

If there's one staple ingredient you'll find in every Tennessee kitchen, it's honey. It's great drizzled on biscuits but it's even better in mead. Yep, you read that right: mead. At Nashville's first meadery, beer yeast is combined with rich honeys from Tennessee hives (some are even here in East Nashville) to make beverages with a truly local flavor. Enjoy a draft in Honeytree's woodsy tasting room before picking up a cork-sealed bottle of mead or a jar of honey.

OLIVE & SINCLAIR CHOCOLATE CO.

Map 3; 1828 Fatherland Street, East Nashville; ///wire.body.acting; www.oliveandsinclair.com

The mouthwatering aromas of roasted cacao nibs and caramel wind through this chocolate shop and factory, luring in dessert fiends. Ethically sourced organic cacao fuels Olive & Sinclair's addictive bars, which each have megawatt flavors: cinnamon chili, coffee crunch, and even candied lemon are available for the taking. Each chocolate bar is packaged in gorgeous vintage-style paper, so it has a really old-school feel – the perfect gift for your mom and pop.

» **Don't leave without** joining a tour of the factory to witness just how much love goes into each bar. And, hallelujah, it ends with a tasting.

THE TURNIP TRUCK

Map 5; 5001 Charlotte Avenue, West Nashville; ///speech.grabs.much; www.theturniptruck.com

Forget about Whole Foods. This grocer is your one-stop-shop for truly local and artisanal food. Our top recommend? Hot Sauce Nashville, a small batch hot sauce made here in town by husband and wife Chris and Chelsea. For every bottle bought, the makers donate a meal to a local food bank.

BANG CANDY COMPANY

Map 2; 1300 Clinton Street I Suite 127, Germantown;
///charms.wells.wool; www.bangcandycompany.com

Bang Candy's shop feels vintage thanks to its location in Marathon Village *(p104)*, but it's big on modern attitude. The confectionery store creates inventive and whimsical treats, like rose cardamom-flavored marshmallows and chocolate bark flecked with popping candy.

BATCH

Map 2; 900 Rosa L. Parks Boulevard, Downtown;
///passes.united.post; www.batchusa.com

While we'll always recommend hitting up local flagship stores, if you're pushed for time and need a gift quick, go straight to Batch. Based in the farmers' market's food hall *(p105)*, the seller specializes in edible treats from around the state and even assembles magnificent gift baskets of all things Nashville (think locally made candy, hot chicken spice, sauces, pancake mix). The lovely folk of Batch are also more than happy to point you in the direction of products from women-, Black- and LGBTQ+-owned businesses – just ask.

KERNELS GOURMET POPCORN

Map 3; 2501 Gallatin Avenue B, East Nashville; ///today.pines.tricks;
www.kernelsnashville.com

Every Christmas, sisters Jennifer, Erica, and Amber got a popcorn tin from their mom and dad and, over the years, the tradition turned into a business idea: Kernels Gourmet Popcorn. The East Nashville poppery turns out perfect little puffs covered in sweet and savory mixes, like "sweet heat," made with caramel, cheese, and "Nashville hot spice," of course. You'll be ordering bulk batches for the holidays after just one mouthful.

NASHVILLE JAM COMPANY

Map 4; 2806 Columbine Place, Berry Hill; ///sleep.animal.unique; www.nashvillejamco.com

It's an age-old problem here in the South: locals can't keep up with the number of fruits and veggies springing up in their verdant gardens. Husband and wife Gary and Cortney resorted to making and selling jams at farmers' markets down in Murfreesboro and, before they knew it, the pair were responsible for a jam sensation. Today, the Nashville Jam Company stocks inventive flavors like strawberry jalapeño, peach habañero, and smoky tomato – the perfect pairing for any carbohydrate.

>> **Don't leave without** stopping in at the café and ordering a big ol' basket of biscuits so you can dive into the jam then and there.

Try it!
BAKE BISCUITS

Want to gift the perfect Southern biscuit? Head to the city's iconic Loveless Cafe and snag a bag of its legendary biscuit mix. It sells biscuit cutters, too *(www. lovelesscafe.com)*.

Vintage Gems

Music City is both glamorous and scrappy, so shopping for vintage here just feels right. Vintage stores channel music industry energy so every shopper is guaranteed to leave looking and feeling like a rockstar.

BLACK SHAG VINTAGE

Map 3; 1220 Gallatin Avenue, East Nashville; ///proper.scouts.guard; www.blackshagvintage.com

Let your inner rock god out at Black Shag Vintage, where you can get fully outfitted in badass bandanas, boots, and band tees. You'll spot Stevie Nicks types checking out waistcoats and young guitar players the spit of Jon Bon Jovi admiring the leather jackets.

THE HIP ZIPPER

Map 3; 1008 Forrest Avenue Suite A, East Nashville; ///winner.reject.goad; www.hipzipper.com

Walk into this humble boutique, tightly packed with rails of vintage clothing, and you'll quickly realize owner Trish is totally obsessed with pre-loved 20th-century fashions. After a 50s pocketbook purse to complete that outfit? Or a 70s crop top for the summer sun? Or an 80s patterned shirt for your man? The Hip Zipper has you covered.

PRE TO POST MODERN

Map 4; 2110 8th Avenue South, Melrose; ///apply.coins.sharp;
(615) 292-1958

Pre to Post is a raucous explosion of color. College students inspect patterned shirts and mini dresses while discerning couples eye sexy (affordable!) mid-century furniture and peruse the vinyl. Everyone exchanges approving looks at the checkout as they grab last-minute tchotchkes at the counter.

>> Don't leave without flicking through the store's vintage vinyl and book selection, both of which include some absolute classics.

STAR STRUCK VINTAGE

Map 3; 604 Gallatin Avenue, Unit 109, East Nashville;
///scarcely.groom.loops; www.starstruckvintage.com

This cavernous store has a great selection of clothes from the 70s, 80s, and 90s but the real find here is the rack of concert tees, straight from the tours of Bowie, Kiss, the Rolling Stones, and Sting. Buy them in their original state or fashionably distressed and dream of rock's glory days.

Try it!
SWING DANCING

Don your newly purchased vintage attire and let your hair down with Swing Dance Nashville. Sign up for a lesson or drop in at the Friday night Big Band dance *(www. swingdancenashville.com)*.

Liked by the locals

"I love when older people pop into the store and say they remember a piece from their parents' house. And I love it when younger people come in and it's all new to them. Visiting is more than shopping – it's an experience."

JEANINE ROBINSON,
OWNER OF DASHWOOD VINTAGE & FLORA

ANTIQUE ARCHAEOLOGY

Map 2; 1300 Clinton Street #130, Marathon Village;
///body.crust.quarrel; www.antiquearchaeology.com

The American Pickers shot to fame after the first episode of their TV show, in which the duo hunt for treasures in barns and backyards across rural America. Thankfully for fans and wannabe collectors, the pickers' latest finds – including cool signage and classic guitars – can be purchased here at their store, housed in an old automobile factory.

SAVANT VINTAGE

Map 4; 2302 12th Avenue South, 12 South; ///rank.struck.forced;
(615) 385-0856

Want to buy vintage that feels undeniably cool? Savant is your stop; it's stuffed floor to ceiling with treasures and clothing with South-western flair (think suede fringed jackets and turquoise jewelry). It's no wonder celebs love it, nor that the store has appeared in *Vogue*.

>> Don't leave without trying on some of the store's gorgeous vintage denim. The neatly arranged rail of jeans is especially tempting.

DASHWOOD VINTAGE & FLORA

Map 6; 2416 Music Valley Drive #115, Opry Mills; ///vibrates.cherry.fines;
www.dashwoodtn.com

It might be found in a somewhat neglected-looking little strip mall but Dashwood, with its restored mid-century armchairs, side tables, desks, and cabinets in shades of gold, caramel, and olive, has all the goods to create your dream home.

Beloved Markets

Nashville loves its markets. You need only look at how many kinds of market there are: outdoor and covered, food and furniture, old and new. Whichever you choose, remember to bring a tote (or five).

MARATHON VILLAGE

Map 2; 1305 Clinton Street, Suite 100, North Nashville; ///first.closes.ticket; www.marathonvillage.net

This cluster of artisan makers and independents is housed in the gorgeous brick warehouses that once accommodated Marathon Motor Works. There's a friendly community vibe to the place; chatting with shopkeepers as you browse home goods, jewelry, antiques, and whiskeys is to be expected here.

Try it!
JEWELRY MAKING

Why not combine a visit to Marathon Village with a workshop? Paige Barbee Jewelry crafts silver pieces inspired by the Victorian era and, with Paige's guidance, you can design your own *(www.paigebarbee.com)*.

MUSIC CITY FLEA

Map 3; 400 Davidson Street, East Nashville; ///reveal.entry.spoon;
www.themarketplacenashville.com

On Saturday, nothing quite beats hanging out at East Nashville's
Music City Flea. This market is all about supporting local makers
and small businesses, a cause Nashvillians passionately embrace.
Young families and groups of students browse the baked goods,
handmade bath products, and locally made jewelry. Even doggies
can leave with a bag of Nashville-made goodies. Once their totes
are full, those in-the-know head out back to the sister market, the
Music City Food Truck Park, which features around ten trucks and,
you guessed it, live music. This is Music City, after all.

NASHVILLE FARMERS' MARKET

Map 2; 900 Rosa L. Parks Boulevard, Downtown; ///purple.trash.paid;
www.nashvillefarmersmarket.org

There isn't anything quite like a farmers' market in the South, and
especially in summertime. Open every day, Nashville Farmers' Market
draws regional growers from miles around to display sumptuous
greens, glistening blackberries, and crimson tomatoes in its open-air
farm sheds. But it's not just a cornucopia of fruit and vegetables.
Bakers and cheesemongers also sell their tempting produce, so
you'll find everything you need to rustle up a delicious Southern-
inspired meal. The market's fairy-lit food court also features local
restaurants and is a good spot for a post-shop beer and bite.

» Don't leave without seeking out the pie vendor, who makes
lip-smacking sweet pies (we're talking pecan, pumpkin, fudge).

PLAZA MARIACHI

Map 6; 3955 Nolensville Pike, South Nashville; ///spits.rams.brick; www.plazamariachi.com

Part-marketplace, part-venue, Plaza Mariachi is all about celebrating cultural diversity. Fill your boots with Latin American goodies (Mexican candies, Venezuelan coffee, and Colombian *arepas*) before watching a *lucha libre* wrestling match or playing a game of Mexican bingo.

EAST NASHVILLE FARMERS' MARKET

Map 3; 511 Woodland Street, East Nashville; ///pencil.insist.drops; www.eastnashvillemarket.com

As the clock strikes lunchtime on Tuesday afternoons, the trendy neighbors of East Nashville have one place on their mind: this crackerjack of a farmers' market. Office workers and gaggles of young friends peruse the pop-up market's tented stalls for foamy

Shh!

Keep your eye out for art and design market Porter Flea (*www.porterflea.com*). It might pop up just a couple of times a year (in summer and around the holidays) but, lord, is it worth the wait. Aimed at tastemakers, the market is all about celebrating the creations of local and mainly young talent. Milliennial makers showcase their tie-dye fashions, emoji- inspired jewelry, illustrative artworks, and vegan leather accessories. You'll have all of your Christmas shopping done in one big swoop.

coffees, ready-to-eat soups, and pasta salads, and stock up on fresh produce for a home-cooked dinner while they're at it. Armed with their loot, they all settle in nearby East Park for their picnic lunch.

L&L MARKETPLACE

Map 5; 3820 Charlotte Avenue, West Nashville; ///skills.works.exit; www.landlmarket.com

L&L Marketplace opened in 2019 though the market building dates back to 1929 when it was a hosiery mill (something new born from something old – how very Nashville). Open Monday through Saturday, the couple of dozen boutiques sell everything from home goods to fresh flowers to artisan foods. It's the domain of friends lunching, who enjoy a bottle and bite at Culture + Co. before a browse of the fresh homeware at The Barefoot Cottage.

» **Don't leave without** buying a pick-me-up latte from Honey Coffee Roasters and a Louisiana crunch pound cake for when you get home.

NASHVILLE FLEA MARKET

Map 4; 500 Wedgewood Avenue, Wedgewood-Houston; ///hurls.plans.diary; (615) 862-5016

A Music City tradition since 1969, Nashville Flea Market fills a warren of warehouses with collectible antiques and pre-loved clothing. Our top tip? Allow plenty of time: there's a lot of stuff to look through here. But don't get it twisted, this ain't a bunch of junk. The browsers' paradise stocks gorgeous vintage furniture, glam fur coats, even diamond rings. Be prepared to bargain and don't forget to bring cash.

Music Stores

You can't visit Music City without buying a piece of music to take home – that might be a pre-loved record, a hot guitar, or a kooky new instrument to learn (mandolin, anyone?).

THIRD MAN RECORDS

Map 1; 623 7th Avenue South, Downtown; ///unless.locate.people; www.thirdmanrecords.com

Third Man Records, owned by Jack White of White Stripes fame, is all about finding wild and wacky ways to get records from its in-house label into the hands of the people. They've dropped vinyl from the sky and put together a band of mechanical monkeys, all to promote up-and-coming artists. At the Third Man HQ in Music

Try it!
RETRO RECORDING

Send an old-school voicemail in Third Man's 1947 Voice-o-Graph recording booth. It records up to two minutes of audio and spits out a phonograph disc you can mail as a unique postcard.

City you can see the Wonka-like shenanigans for yourself, pick up a record from an emerging band, or see a show in the store's beloved Blue Room venue.

PHONOLUXE RECORDS

Map 4; 2609 Nolensville Pike, South Nashville; ///hush.battle.caged; (615) 259-3500

While we love that vinyl is mainstream again, there's nothing like a *High Fidelity* style record shop where the staff are in the business because they're genuine, obsessive music nerds. Phonoluxe is that shop. Only open on weekends, this stalwart is where die-hard collectors, young and old, flock to see what pre-loved records (country, blues, jazz, folk, and rock) the team have acquired that week.

CARTER VINTAGE GUITARS

Map 1; 625 8th Avenue South, Downtown; ///river.wonderfully.jumpy; www.cartervintage.com

One of the country's best-known guitar shops, Carter was founded by husband and wife Walter and Christine, who each bring a whopping 25 years of experience in the vintage guitar business. Stop by for a chitchat with the duo and browse their extensive guitar collection, which includes old, new, and rare instruments. Musicians absolutely love Carter, so don't be surprised if you bump into someone you saw on stage the night before.

» Don't leave without asking the staff about the celebrity-owned guitars, like Ed King's Strat that he played on "Sweet Home Alabama."

GRIMEY'S

Map 3; 1060 East Trinity Lane, East Nashville;
///ballots.food.hammer; www.grimeys.com

You'll feel like a kid in a candy shop at Nashville's go-to record shop. Grimey's has everything a music lover could possibly ask for – from punk to prog, soul to soft jazz, new and used records, big names and emerging local artists. The fun doesn't stop at retail therapy, either; check the website for upcoming record release shows where you can catch an artist playing their album live at the store.

» Don't leave without checking out the store's collection of books, magazines, and movies, which all rotate around a music theme.

VINYL TAP

Map 3; 2038 Greenwood Avenue, East Nashville;
///cliff.splice.head; www.vinyltapnashville.com

This is the kind of place that makes you ask, "Why did no one think of this sooner?" Vinyl Tap is a combo of a record store and bar, where you can order a beer and flip through a selection of new and classic records. Staff picks play in the background as you sip and shop.

FANNY'S HOUSE OF MUSIC

Map 3; 1101 Holly Street, East Nashville; ///debate.craft.roses;
www.fannyshouseofmusic.com

One of the few female-owned music stores in town, Fanny's is intended to be a place where male and female musicians feel comfortable shopping, playing, and working together. Sure, there's

 Fanny's music lessons cost just $30–55, so you can buy and learn to play your new strings in one swoop. | all the standard guitars, amps, microphones, and accessories here but there's also folk instruments like mandolins, banjos, and dobros.

FORK'S DRUM CLOSET

Map 4; 308 Chestnut Street, Chestnut Hill; ///books.tilt.woke; www.forksdrumcloset.com

A candy store for drummers, Fork's is all about percussion. Budding Dave Grohls and John Bonhams comb the store's rows of sticks and cymbals, drum heads and tambourines, looking for the perfect new additions to update their kit. Newbie drummers, don't sweat it: the staff are incredibly knowledgeable and endlessly patient. They'll walk you through everything you need to know, and will encourage you to have a play in-house. Shop dog Mel will likely also come say hello.

RUMBLE SEAT MUSIC

Map 4; 1805 8th Avenue South, 8th Avenue; ///proud.still.create; www.rumbleseatmusic.com

Play a few licks on a guitar that's sure to have a storied history at 8th Avenue's Rumble Seat Music, a top dealer of vintage gear and guitars. The collection here is prolific – you'll find rare Les Pauls from the 50s that cost more than a house, along with more affordable additions for your growing collection. Owner Eliot Michael has quite the musical history himself, having played New York's underground scene in the rockin' 60s and 70s.

0 meters 250
0 yards 250

12TH AVE SOUTH

10TH AVE SOUTH

ASHWOOD AVENUE

LINDEN AVENUE

**Browse for a gift at
SERENDIPITY**

Discover unique and ethical goods, like
t-shirts printed with eco-friendly ink and
jewelry made by survivors of sex trafficking.

1

**Find a new outfit at
EMERSON GRACE**

2

Stop by this airy women's boutique where
owner and former fashion exec Kimberly
handpicks each stylish piece. Don't miss
"The Local Focus" section, which
highlights regional indie designers.

*Fashion boutique
HERO is run by stylist
Claudia Robertson
Fowler and attracts
clients like Faith Hill and
Martina McBride.*

BELMONT BOULEVARD

SWEETBRIAR AVENUE

12 SOUTH

3

**Up your jeans game at
IMOGENE + WILLIE**

Looking for the perfect pair of jeans?
This husband-and-wife-run shop, in
an old gas station, crafts high-quality,
custom-made denim. It's a must-visit.

MONTROSE AVENUE

*The **Looking Pretty,
Music City** mural, by
artist Emily Eisenhart,
was a 2019 collaboration
with clothing store
Madewell.*

12TH AVE SOUTH

4

**Stop for a bite at
BURGER UP**

Refuel with a specialty burger
made with ingredients sourced
from local farms.

10TH AVENUE SOUTH

KIRKWOOD AVENUE

**Explore curated goodies at
WHITE'S MERCANTILE**

5

Fill your basket with gorgeous
handcrafted candles, kitchenware,
and toiletries at this "general store
for the modern tastemaker."

KIRKWOOD AVENUE

*Sevier
Park*

A morning of
indie shopping

Forget fast fashion. Here in Nashville, big brands take a backseat to artisan makers, social enterprises, and eco-conscious entrepreneurs. And nowhere is this felt more than in 12 South, a residential neighborhood with a charming half-mile stretch of indie shops that are steeped in Nashville's altruistic spirit. Stroll down the area's eponymous 12th Avenue South and stock up on goodies for your home and closet, all the while supporting small business owners, who you just might meet as you shop.

1. Serendipity
2301 12th Avenue South;
www.serendipity12th.com
///novel.ranks.than

2. Emerson Grace
2304 12th Avenue South;
www.emersongrace
nashville.com
///head.congratulations.scale

3. Imogene + Willie
2601 12th Avenue South;
www.imogeneandwillie.com
///angel.games.things

4. Burger Up
2901 12th Avenue South;
www.burger-up.com
///match.slides.cycles

5. White's Mercantile
2908 12th Avenue South;
www.whitesmercantile.com
///shots.scrap.audio

HERO
////unless.bleak.renew

**Looking Pretty,
Music City**
///badly.public.never

ARTS & CULTURE

"The Athens of the South," Nashville is packed with museums, galleries, theaters, and music venues that offer an insight into Music City's exceptional story.

Musical Legacy

*They don't call it Music City for nothing. Dive into
Nashville's musical history by learning the stories
behind the songs and visiting the venues where
the artists became legends.*

NATIONAL MUSEUM OF AFRICAN AMERICAN MUSIC

Map 1; 510 Broadway, Downtown; ///hike.ports.hang; www.nmaam.org

Your favorite song probably wouldn't exist if it weren't for Black artistry – jazz, blues, soul, rock 'n' roll, and even country all evolved from African American traditions. This eye-opening museum celebrates the pioneers behind more than 50 genres, with interactive exhibits that let you improvise with a jazz band, sing with a choir, and create your own music to take home.

THE RYMAN

Map 1; 116 5th Avenue North, Downtown; ///shout.means.deal;

www.ryman.com

Known as "The Mother Church," the Ryman makes even seasoned musicians (it's hosted everyone from Elvis to Taylor Swift) feel a little emotional. It began as an actual church – stained-glass windows line

Check the floor plan to avoid ending up with an obstructed view. The balcony has some of the best seats. | the walls and guests sit on pews – and the intimate atmosphere still has a spiritual feel, creating an electrifying connection between the artist and audience.

JOHNNY CASH MUSEUM

Map 1; 119 3rd Avenue South, Downtown; ///output.cases.often; www.johnnycashmuseum.com

If you think a museum dedicated to one artist sounds dull, think again. Join Johnny Cash devotees of all ages for an inside look at the life and career of the Man in Black. Featuring personal memorabilia, from his awards to his Bible, the exhibits bring you face to face with a musician who was incredibly talented, perfectly flawed, and beautifully human.

» Don't leave without also visiting the Patsy Cline Museum upstairs to learn about one of country music's most influential female vocalists.

COUNTRY MUSIC HALL OF FAME

Map 1; 222 Republican John Lewis Way South, Downtown; ///grabs.frames.bind; www.countrymusichalloffame.org

Country music is so much more than twang, trucks, and heartbreak. For proof, just look to this massive museum – it covers everything you could possibly want to know about the genre, and then some. A place of pilgrimage for superfans and curious Nashville visitors alike, it's got two floors of fashion, instruments, memorabilia, and educational exhibits in which you can lose yourself for hours.

GRAND OLE OPRY

Map 6; 2804 Opryland Drive, Opryland; ///burn.burst.spoon;
www.opry.com

Nashville wouldn't be Nashville without the Grand Ole Opry. This weekly concert, broadcast live on the radio since 1925, has launched the careers of countless country music stars. Attending the show is a treasured ritual for fans, with families, young couples, and grandparents all gathering to watch the performances. Diehards can add on a backstage tour to learn what happens behind the scenes.

HISTORIC RCA STUDIO B

Map 5; 1611 Roy Acuff Place, Midtown; ///pints.fans.impose;
www.studiob.org

There's something magical about a classic recording studio. The walls emit a palpable energy, infused with the memory of creative passion and the unseen moments between takes. And there are few studios more classic than RCA Studio B, the birthplace of the "Nashville Sound." Stand on the spot that Elvis stood, discover why Dolly Parton is a business genius, and understand how Nashville became Music City.

JEFFERSON STREET SOUND

Map 2; 2004 Jefferson Street, North Nashville; ///common.unions.edge;
www.jeffersonstreetsound.com/museum

During the mid-20th century, Jefferson Street was a thriving Black business district with clubs hosting the likes of Jimi Hendrix and Etta James. City politics and racially disparate development eventually broke up the community here, but Jefferson Street Sound ensures that its legacy is not forgotten. The museum offers tours by appointment to those in-the-know, revealing what made this area the place to be.

>> Don't leave without asking if founder Lorenzo Washington is in the house and free to share first-hand stories from the heyday.

MUSICIANS HALL OF FAME AND MUSEUM

Map 2; 401 Gay Street, Downtown; ///scan.bands.hopes;
www.musicianshalloffame.com

Sure, you know who sings on your favorite records, but do you know who plays on them? The Musicians Hall of Fame and Museum is a tribute to the talented session players and background vocalists who made the songs you love so special. Inside, are exhibits on famous studios like Fame, Motown, and Stax, with memorabilia, and stories from artists who recorded at each one. You'll walk away with a newfound musical expertise that's bound to wow your friends the next time "Ain't Too Proud to Beg" or "You Got It" comes on the radio.

Try it!
SING A CLASSIC

Want to record your own masterwork? At the Ryman *(p116)* you can choose from 22 songs, sung by the likes of Elvis, Johnny Cash, and Patsy Cline, and record a cover version to take home for just $15.

City History

It's not just music that's left its mark on Nashville. The city has a past as a Civil War battleground, an incubator for the Civil Rights movement, and a bastion of education. Uncover its tales of tragedy and triumph.

TENNESSEE STATE MUSEUM

Map 2; 1000 Rosa L. Parks Boulevard, Downtown; ///anyone.drives.deals; www.tnmuseum.org

Residing in a sparkly modern building, the Tennessee State Museum takes visitors on an exhaustively researched journey through the state's intricate past. This might sound heavy going, but the varied exhibits are utterly absorbing – especially those on the state's Native American history, which is a topic that goes unexplored all too often. And even better: it's all free.

FISK UNIVERSITY

Map 2; 1000 17th Avenue North, North Nashville; ///divide.sparks.brief; www.fisk.edu

Known as the "Athens of the South," Nashville is home to dozens of higher education institutions, many of which have profoundly shaped its history. The Fisk School was established just six months after the conclusion of the Civil War – making it the oldest university in Nashville – and its first students were people of all ages who had formerly been enslaved. Today it remains an influential institution on the local and national level, and its famed Jubilee Singers – who started as a traveling musical troupe to raise money for the university back in the 1870s – continue to garner accolades, winning their first Grammy in 2021. Take a walk through the grounds to learn about the school's impact on Nashville and the country as a whole – the campus is a National Historic District, and is littered with informative plaques.

» **Don't leave without** heading a block west to visit the memorial to the 1960 Looby House Bombing, a pivotal event in local Civil Rights history.

UNITED STREET TOURS

Map 1; 150 4th Avenue North, Downtown; ///tunnel.brave.dart;
www.unitedstreettours.com

Black history is Nashville history, though many tours and museums abbreviate it to a mere footnote. United Street Tours founder Chakita Patterson is looking to change that, with guided routes designed to inspire dedication to social justice in Nashville and beyond – itineraries focus on the city's extensive Civil Rights history, the history of its Black communities and institutions, and the impact of Black citizens on Nashville's growth and development. Our pick is the Black Neighborhood Tour: learn about the rhythm and blues heritage of Jefferson Street and support small Black-owned businesses and artists along the way. Skip the plantation tours and #WalkUnited instead.

DOWNTOWN PRESBYTERIAN CHURCH

Map 1; 154 5th Avenue North, Downtown; ///slang.again.wider;
www.dpchurch.com

A chimeric product of historical events, the Downtown Presbyterian Church is a unique stop for any history buff. Originally built as a house of worship in 1814, it burned down twice before taking its present-day form, with construction and remodeling lasting from 1849 until the 1880s. Over the decades it was used as a Civil War hospital, a shelter for flood victims, and housing for soldiers on leave in Nashville during World War II. Book a tour on a Tuesday or Thursday to learn about the church's history and marvel at its somewhat peculiar interior, which was built in what was termed the Egyptian Revival style (read: very groovy).

>> Don't leave without popping into the Browsing Room, which showcases works by the church's artists-in-residence (yes, would you believe there are artists studios' hidden away in the church).

FORT NEGLEY

Map 4; 1100 Fort Negley Boulevard, Downtown; ///before.faced.barks;
www.nashville.gov/Parks-and-Recreation

Because of its status as an important economic hub, Nashville was one of the first Confederate cities to be captured by the Union during the Civil War. Fort Negley, the Civil War's biggest inland fort, was built by Union forces and conscripted laborers (primarily people who had formerly been enslaved) on the top of St. Cloud Hill, making it a formidable post that succeeded in repelling Confederate advances. Today, visitors can walk among the ruins,

Head here at sunset when the stunning views of the city skyline are at their most striking.

passing through walkways, over defense walls, and around gun turrets. The fort has a small visitor center and plenty of plaques relaying the site's history.

BICENTENNIAL CAPITOL MALL STATE PARK

Map 2; 600 James Robertson Parkway, Downtown; ///client.books.tune; www.tnstateparks.com/parks/bicentennial-mall

Look closely at the sprawling lawn of this urban park and you'll find the city's history literally etched into its stone. Granite maps of the state outline important elements of Tennessee, from geological features to musical influences. There's even a hint of the future here, too: buried beneath the markers along the Walkway of Counties are sealed time capsules, waiting to be opened at the tercentennial in 2096.

NASHVILLE PUBLIC LIBRARY

Map 1; 615 Church Street, Downtown; ///senior.lungs.system; www.library.nashville.org/locations/main-library

Along with Montgomery, Birmingham, and Selma, Nashville played a crucial role in the Civil Rights movement – student activists received non-violent protest training here, and went on to participate in the Nashville sit-ins and the Freedom Rides. This important era of the city's history is documented in the Nashville Public Library's Civil Rights Room, where timelines, video exhibits, and books provide a deeper insight into the fight for human rights.

Favorite Museums

With all the music, art, and history that's flowed through Nashville, it's only natural that the city wants to celebrate it. Cue an impressive roster of museums, covering everything from vintage cars to modern art.

LANE MOTOR MUSEUM

Map 6; 702 Murfreesboro Pike, South Nashville; ///deck.farm.ruins; www.lanemotormuseum.org

The passion project of automobile collector Jeff Lane, this little museum is a joy to visit, even if you don't give two hoots about cars. It features a rotating assembly of eclectic vehicles from all over the world, including futuristic concept cars, slick racing machines, and a giant World War II-era amphibious vehicle. Unleash your inner gearhead and marvel at decades of design and engineering.

THE PARTHENON

Map 5; 2500 West End Avenue, West End; ///animal.flap.dated; www.nashvilleparthenon.com

Why is there a full-size replica of the Parthenon in the middle of a Nashville park, you ask? Well, it was built as part of the Tennessee Centennial Exposition in 1897, as a tribute to Nashville's nickname, the "Athens of the South." Head inside to find displays about the building's history and explore a pair of art galleries with temporary exhibitions that cover topics such as ancient technologies and contemporary photography.

» **Don't leave without** taking a walk through the rest of Centennial Park, where there's a weekly Musicians Corner on summer Saturdays.

ADVENTURE SCIENCE CENTER

Map 4; 800 Fort Negley Boulevard, Downtown; ///wiring.leap.lazy; www.adventuresci.org

With a glowing, color-changing pyramid on its roof, the Adventure Science Center is a beacon to the city's science fans. Sure, during the day this is the domain of kids – activities like crawling through an oversized heart and piloting a fighter jet simulator keep them enthralled for hours – but the museum knows that its young visitors don't disappear, they just grow up. Events to reignite your childlike wonder include regular laser shows in the planetarium, as well as adult-only nights complete with alcohol. Cheers to that.

Try it!
YOGA IN SPACE

If you fancy a far-out twist on your daily yoga practice, sign up for the Adventure Science Center's Yoga Under the Stars. Classes are held in the planetarium, beneath the majestic Milky Way.

FISK UNIVERSITY GALLERIES

**Map 2; 1000 17th Avenue North, North Nashville; ///friday.tigers.error;
www.fiskuniversitygalleries.org**

Fisk has a long legacy of supporting the arts. The university's Art
Department here was founded by Harlem Renaissance pioneer
Aaron Douglas, and notable names such as David Driskell,
Stephanie Pogue, and Terry Adkins have all passed through its
doors. Their work and that of other alumni can be found among the
university's permanent art collection, which is displayed in rotating
exhibits in the Carl Van Vechten and Aaron Douglas galleries.
Interestingly, the 4,000-strong collection also includes a number of
high-profile works once owned by photographer Alfred Stieglitz.
These were donated after his death – to the surprise of many – by
his wife, artist Georgia O' Keeffe, who knew then Fisk president
Charles S. Johnson through writer Carl Van Vechten.

» **Don't leave without** stopping by Cravath Hall to see the striking
murals by Aaron Douglas, which portray a vivid narrative history of
African American life.

FRIST ART MUSEUM

**Map 1; 919 Broadway, Downtown; ///chip.assets.entire;
www.fristartmuseum.org**

Who'd have thought this palatial Art Deco dream of a museum
used to be a post office? Today it serves a much more creative
purpose as the preeminent art gallery in town, with an outstanding
program of international exhibitions making stops in Nashville while
on tour. Past subjects have included work by Frida Kahlo, Nick Cave,

Alphonse Mucha, Pablo Picasso, and even ancient sculptures from Rome. The museum's summertime Frist Fridays are a big draw with the Downtown TGIF crowd, who flock here to explore the exhibitions and enjoy live outdoor concerts, drinks in hand.

TENNESSEE SPORTS HALL OF FAME

Map 1; 501 Broadway, Downtown; ///driver.cars.mice; www.tshf.net

Like many Southern states, Tennessee takes immense pride in its sports legacy; Nashville itself is home to NFL and NHL teams, and it recently added an MLS team to the roster. This encyclopedic museum honors over 500 Tennesseans who have made an impact on the court, field, and rink – including athletes, coaches, sports writers, and broadcasters – making for a great afternoon immersed in the state's sports history. One visit here and you'll run away with the sports category at any local trivia night.

Shh!

We can all agree that art and artifacts don't just belong in museums. Take the Joseph (*www.josephnashville.com*), a seriously stylish hotel in SoBro that's decked out with artworks old and new. Few realize that these include pieces lent by the Pizzuti Collection of the Columbus Museum of Art in Ohio, where hotel owner Joseph Pizzuti hails from. And you don't need a room here to enjoy them – sip a coffee in the bar and admire the colorful chandelier by Mischa Kahn.

Contemporary Art

Nashville's contemporary art scene is bursting with energy – especially during the monthly neighborhood art crawls, when galleries lay on special events. Join the party or devise your own tour of the best local art.

THE ARCADE

Map 1; 65 Arcade Alley, Downtown; ///basket.square.cure; (615) 248-6673

Hidden among Downtown's closely packed buildings, the Arcade feels like a bit of an outlier. Built in 1902, it was modeled on the Galleria Vittorio Emanuele II in Milan, Italy, and today it contrasts sharply with the architecture around it. The first floor features a handful of small mom-and-pop shops with an old Nashville quality

Try it!
PAINT YOUR OWN

Feeling inspired? Head to Dabble Studio *(www.dabbleevents.com)* to flex those artist muscles in one of its painting classes. All skill levels are welcome and you can even bring your own wine to sip while you create.

about them, while the second floor houses dozens of contemporary art galleries. Each one is distinctly original, and all come alive for the monthly Downtown Art Crawl.

ZEITGEIST ART GALLERY

**Map 4; 516 Hagan Street #100, Wedgewood-Houston;
///soda.helps.beats; www.zeitgeist-art.com**

There's a big-city-art vibe at this large, airy gallery on the industrial side of Wedgewood-Houston. Works exhibited here are daring, intelligent, and sometimes discomfiting – it's likely you'll be thinking about them long after you've departed. Add in a regular program of live events such as talks, dance exhibitions, and music performances, and it's of little surprise that Zeitgeist is an ever-popular stop on the Wedgewood-Houston Art Crawl.

RED ARROW GALLERY

**Map 3; 919 Gallatin Avenue, East Nashville; ///fish.pulse.debit;
www.theredarrowgallery.com**

Red Arrow Gallery champions artists early in their careers, giving them a gorgeous, airy venue to show off their talents. On the first Saturday of the month, it opens up its big garage door to welcome art hounds with music, drinks, and good vibes. And the gallery is but one part of the artist enclave in which it is housed – neighbors include a woodworking studio, a recording studio, and a guitar maker.

» Don't leave without snapping a photo beneath Nashville's riff on the Hollywood sign (Howdywoo), next to the Soft Junk recording studio.

ELEPHANT GALLERY

**Map 2; 1411 Buchanan Street, North Nashville; ///tricky.scars.meant;
www.elephantgallery.com**

This oddball studio and gallery goes all in when it comes to its
exhibitions (painting walls, installing carpets, you name it), making
the art-viewing experience a welcome breath of fresh air in a sea of
white-walled spaces. Featured works are primarily by regional artists,
and regularly include oversized sculptures and wacky ceramics.

21C MUSEUM HOTEL

**Map 1; 221 2nd Avenue North, Downtown; ///radar.vent.ripe;
www.21cmuseumhotels.com/nashville**

Created to bring modern art to cities where it may have been
lacking, 21c hotels function as both inspiring places to stay and
edgy local art galleries. Nashville's 21c is a gorgeous space that
displays anything from video installations to taxidermy.

» Don't leave without enjoying an arty meal at the Gray and
Dudley, 21c's atmospheric restaurant and bar.

ONE DROP INK

**Map 2; 1511 Jefferson Street, North Nashville; ///handed.gained.fuels;
www.onedropink.com**

Thanks to the tireless work of owner Elisheba Israel Mrozik, this
hybrid art gallery and tattoo shop has become a cultural hub in
North Nashville. It hosts shows, artisan pop-ups, drawing classes,
and talks – all intended to champion local emerging artists.

Liked by the locals

"I am always creating. Everything I've learned, I'm happy to share with any artist who comes in."

ELISHEBA ISRAEL MROZIK,
ONE DROP INK OWNER, ARTIST,
AND COMMUNITY ARTS ACTIVIST

Street Murals

As street art has become ever more popular worldwide, Nashville has wholeheartedly embraced bringing art to the public in every corner of the city. Here are some of the standouts.

ONE DAY, I WILL RESCUE YOUR BROTHER TOO

Map 1; 204 6th Avenue North, Downtown; ///pounds.tries.buyers

This striking mural from German duo Herakut requires a few looks to fully take in the whole story – a large dog holds a young girl while a boy remains in a cage, flipping the idea of pet adoption completely on its head. Commissioned as part of the Nashville Walls Project, an art initiative designed to bring murals from local and international artists to life, it's one of the most arresting works in the city.

I BELIEVE IN NASHVILLE

Map 4; 2702 12th Avenue South, 12 South; ///moons.become.voting

If you want a local mural with a strong sense of place, this is the one. Painted by Nashville native Adrien Saporiti, the popular design – which plays on the Tennessee state flag – has become something of a city symbol since it first appeared in this alley. It's been replicated

Learn more about the mural, and others, on a Nashville Mural Tour *(www.nashville muraltours.com)*.

in various locations, most notably on the side of Basement East, where it survived the March 2020 tornado (though the rest of the building did not).

HILLSBORO VILLAGE DRAGON

Map 5; 21st Avenue and Belcourt Avenue, Hillsboro Village; ///admits.supper.jaws

Originally painted in 1995 by David Glick and Adam Randolph as part of a community art initiative incorporating the work of elementary school students, the Hillsboro Village Dragon is one of the oldest murals in Nashville. This old-timer got a refresh from local artist Andee Rudloff in 2015, but it maintains its worn-in charm. And why a dragon? It's an ode to a marvelous mosaic dragon in nearby Fannie Mae Dees Park, created by artist Pedro Silva in 1981.

» Don't leave without checking what's on at the Belcourt Theatre across the street; it's been screening movies since the silent era.

OFF THE WALL NASHVILLE

Map 5; 3020 Charlotte Avenue, West Nashville; ///blast.speech.paying

It would be a crime to leave a canvas like this giant wall devoid of color. Just as well, then, that the artists behind Off the Wall have teamed up with local non-profits to create an enormous community-centered piece of art. Founded in the tradition of truly ephemeral street art, this 1,200-ft (365-m) stretch of murals is constantly evolving with pieces that reflect the beauty and diversity of the neighborhood.

DOLLY PARTON

Map 3; 1006 Forrest Avenue, East Nashville; ///plank.hurray.soap

Dolly Parton is Tennessee's patron saint, and for good reason – her literacy program here has been hugely impactful and, of course, she's one of the greatest singer-songwriters in music history. Artist Kim Radford was already working on her depiction of Dolly when the queen of country music so eloquently voiced her support of the Black Lives Matter movement: "Of course Black lives matter. Do we think our little white a**es are the only ones that matter?" And with that, her words are now immortalized on the wall of the 5 Spot *(p153)*.

WHAT LIFTS YOU

Map 1; 302 11th Avenue South, The Gulch; ///evenly.gaps.bonds

Love 'em or hate 'em, the What Lifts You wings by Kelsey Montague are a Nashville icon and a bona fide social media phenomenon. These large, lacy wings are perfectly situated so folks can "wear" them, and many a bachelorette party has paused here to photograph their bride as she takes flight from her single life. Not only is Montague's work a hit in Nashville (this isn't her only piece in town), but the hype has made it overseas – her murals can be found on five continents.

SILO MURAL

Map 5; 1499 51st Avenue North, The Nations; ///sulk.tinsel.tunnel

Painted by Australian artist Guido van Helten, the evocative Silo Mural spurs some obvious questions. Who is this man? And how did van Helten make the piece so dang enormous? The answer to the first is Lee Estes, a nonagenarian who has called The Nations home since the 1920s. And the answer to the second? A 155-ft (47-m) crane was brought in to create the portrait, which spans 15 stories up the side of an old grain silo.

» Don't leave without stopping by the Nations Wall on California Avenue, a tribute to the neighborhood by 11 different artists.

FAMILY MATTERS

Map 2; 26th Avenue and Clarksville Pike, North Nashville; ///dozed.acted.legal

North Nashville served as a base for many activists in the Civil Rights movement, and this powerhouse of a mural by the Norf Art Collective pays tribute to that history. Employing bright, warm colors, it depicts four pivotal social justice figures – Diane Nash, John Lewis, Curlie McGruder, and Alexander Looby – alongside two children who symbolize the continuation of the journey to freedom.

Shh!

It's not just *Family Matters* in North Nashville, you know. Few walking tours head to this largely residential neighborhood, but we're letting you in on the secret. In 2019, the Frist *(p126)* partnered with local artists to create new artworks across the district as part of the Murals of North Nashville Now exhibition. Search on the Frist's website for a map of the works and embark on your own tour – you'll have the murals all to yourself. Bliss.

Performing Arts

Nashville isn't just down-home stages and music bars – it's got beautiful performing arts spaces, and lots of 'em. Put on your going-out duds and enjoy the best of the city's dance productions, plays, and operas.

DARKHORSE THEATER

Map 5; 4610 Charlotte Avenue, Sylvan Park; ///whites.lungs.papers; www.darkhorsetheater.com

Impress a pal with a night of alternative theater in a cozy old church. Darkhorse is a progressive playhouse that creates avenues for up-and-coming writers and actors, staging original works like *Six Triple Eight*, about the first all-Black female battalion in World War II. The space is shared between several companies, so if plays aren't your thing, stop by for a dance, multimedia, or musical show instead.

SCHERMERHORN SYMPHONY CENTER

Map 1; 1 Symphony Place, Downtown; ///enjoy.speak.slang; www.nashvillesymphony.org

The Nashville Symphony isn't your average orchestra. Yes, they play plenty of Mozart and Beethoven, but they also have fun with a creative merging of old and new. Shows at their striking Downtown home range from the music of David Bowie and Led Zeppelin to movie scores and holiday-inspired theme nights. Get dressed up and treat yourself and a date to a night of cultural refinement – no one's judging if that means watching violinists play the opening theme to *Star Wars*.

>> Don't leave without wandering the halls of the Schermerhorn, which have a modern-meets-classical design that matches the music.

TENNESSEE PERFORMING ARTS CENTER

Map 1; 505 Deaderick Street, Downtown; ///dive.update.veal; www.tpac.org
Also known as TPAC, this chic cultural center hosts a wide range of performing arts shows, including touring concerts, plays, comedy shows, and dance productions; it's also home to the well regarded Nashville Ballet, which regularly presents truly boundary-pushing works of art. With three different theater spaces inside the main building, as well as the War Memorial Auditorium across the street, it's always a reliable option when the folks are in town.

Try it!
DANCE WITH THE PROS

The Nashville Ballet (*www.nashvilleballet. com*) hosts a wide range of community classes at its training facility in West Nashville – don your slippers and learn from the professionals.

Liked by the locals

"There's no better place to experience the best in local and indie cinema than the Belcourt Theatre. Come for the films, but you'll quickly realize the charm of this place goes far beyond the screen. It ties together the local community and a creative culture."

DAVE DICICCO, NASHVILLE FILMMAKER

BELCOURT THEATRE

Map 5; 2102 Belcourt Avenue, Hillsboro Village;
///trunk.faster.leans; www.belcourt.org

Film fans and music buffs come together at the Belcourt, a vintage movie theater and nonprofit where you can catch a mix of indie flicks, music documentaries, and classic films. Intellectuals gravitate toward the one-off screenings and live Q&As with filmmakers, but midnight showings of childhood favorites prove this place is for everyone.

NASHVILLE OPERA

Map 5; 3622 Redmon Street, Sylvan Park; ///scars.shed.finds;
www.nashvilleopera.org

Country music hogs the spotlight, but Nashville's music scene is hugely diverse. So why not try something a bit different, and spend a night with the Nashville Opera? You can catch them at Sylvan Park campus, performing both old favorites and fresh creations.

OZ ARTS NASHVILLE

Map 6; 6172 Cockrill Bend Circle, The Nations;
///plates.newscasts.unopened; www.ozartsnashville.org

Housed in a former cigar warehouse, OZ is at the cutting edge of Nashville's dance and theater scene. The program here aims to push boundaries and start conversations, and shows such as *Sloppy Bonnie: A Roadkill Musical for the Modern Chick* will certainly get you gabbing.

» **Don't leave without** checking out the center's visual arts gallery, as well as the curious sculptures dotted around the grounds.

A day of musical history
in Downtown

Think of Downtown and you'll likely picture its famous music stages, honky-tonks, and dance floors – the backdrop for many a night out. But this thriving music scene goes way back and is rooted in deep cultural traditions that started right here. There are few better ways to spend a day than exploring Nashville's incredible music legacy and getting to know the people – past and present – who keep Music City rocking.

1. Sun Diner
105 3rd Avenue South;
www.sundinernashville.com
///second.edge.scrap

2. The Country Music Hall of Fame
222 Republican John Lewis Way South; www.country musichalloffame.org
///grabs.frames.bind

3. Ernest Tubb Record Shop
417 Broadway;
www.ernesttubb.com
///festivity.zeal.rungs

4. Puckett's
500 Church Street;
www.puckettsgro.com
///guides.squad.count

5. The Ryman
116 5th Avenue North;
www.ryman.com
///shout.means.deal

Music City Walk of Fame
///gent.chip.loops

Tuck into meat and three at PUCKETT'S

Stop in for a casual lunch at Puckett's, a Southern comfort food restaurant that started in an old grocery store. If you stay later, you might catch some live music.

4

Catch a show at THE RYMAN

Soak in the energy and the incredible acoustics at this, one of the world's most iconic music venues, which stages local and national acts.

5

Start the day at SUN DINER

Fuel up with a waffle or omelet at this vintage-style diner, which pays homage to the famous Sun Studios where Elvis, Jerry Lee Lewis, and other rockabilly stars got their start.

1

DOWNTOWN

Pick up an album at ERNEST TUBB RECORD SHOP

Grand Ole Opry star Ernest Tubb opened this country vinyl store in 1947, and it's still going strong today. It's impossible to leave empty-handed.

3

Walk of Fame Park

*The **Music City Walk of Fame** honors artists who have made their mark on 200 years of music, like a cappella ensemble the Fisk Jubilee Singers.*

See the stars at THE COUNTRY MUSIC HALL OF FAME

Spend a few hours learning all about the history of country music, its most famous players, and how the Nashville sound came to be.

2

Cumberland River

Riverfront Park

CHURCH STREET
2ND AVENUE NORTH
1ST AVENUE NORTH
3RD AVENUE NORTH
4TH AVE NORTH
REP. JOHN LEWIS WAY NORTH
COMMERCE STREET
BROADWAY
REP. JOHN LEWIS WAY SOUTH
3RD AVENUE SOUTH
DEMONBREUN STREET

0 meters		200
0 yards		200

NIGHTLIFE

As the sun sets over Nashville, the fun is just getting started. Night owls flock to the city's music bars and honky-tonks looking to get footloose and fancy-free.

Honky-Tonkin'

Locals might hate on the notoriously touristy honky-tonks, but they're also the first place they take their out-of-town friends. Join them for a a uniquely Nashville night of honky-tonkin' on Broadway.

THE STAGE ON BROADWAY

Map 1; 412 Broadway, Downtown; ///legal.cards.voter; www.thestageonbroadway.com

Honky-tonks tend to follow a similar formula: western vibes, live country covers, and cold beers. Take the Stage, which has an old saloon feel thanks to its huge wooden bar and epic oil painting *The Highwayman* (it once hung in the home of country singer Waylon Jennings). Honky-tonk hallmarks aside, this hangout really does promise a great night out thanks to the foot-tappingly good country bands that grace the venue's stage.

TOOTSIE'S ORCHID LOUNGE

Map 1; 422 Broadway, Downtown; ///when.salsa.tunes; www.tootsies.net

As the oldest honky-tonk in Nashville, Tootsie's has seen a lot of boots walk through its purple door – the likes of Willie Nelson's, Kris Kristofferson's, and modern stars who still sneak out the back door of the Ryman *(p116)* for a post-show cold one. Hattie Louise "Tootsie" Bess bought the place back in 1960, before paying for the building to be repainted – the decorator mistakenly painted the place orchid purple, an unmissable shade that's become a part of the honky-tonk's identity. Tootsie famously supported struggling artists (she had a cigar box filled with IOUs for unpaid drinks), and little has changed since; up-and-coming country musicians still perform here today.

» **Don't leave without** taking in the countless photographs of musicians who chased their dreams here in Music City.

WILDHORSE SALOON

Map 1; 120 2nd Avenue North, Downtown; ///just.jazz.film; www.wildhorsesaloon.com

Feel like dancing? Make for Wildhorse Saloon, where row upon row of suited and booted locals dance their troubles away. This honky-tonk is truly gigantic, with a vast stage and Opry-like viewing balcony (the ideal spot for those who are less inclined to do-si-do). Reward your boot scootin' with a Yee-Haw IPA and BBQ fare.

Try it!
LINE DANCING

Prefer to walk the line, or dance it? If the latter, learn a few moves with a free line dancing lesson at Wildhorse Saloon, where walk-in masterclasses take place every day 5–8:30pm.

ROBERT'S WESTERN WORLD

Map 1; 416 Broadway B, Downtown; ///noses.venues.hired;
www.robertswesternworld.com

Invite a local to go for a night out on Lower Broadway and you'll
probably get some major side eye, but say you're going to Robert's
and they'll light up. The western-themed bar has been a stalwart for
decades, loved for its famous wall of cowboy boots, nightly rockin'
music, and lack of cover charge. Join grandparents in their vests
and cowboy boots as they two-step to the house band, and groups
of whippersnappers gathering around the bar for guys' or gals' night.
» Don't leave without ordering the "recession special" – a fried
bologna sandwich, chips, beer, and a moon pie for just $6.

NUDIE'S HONKY TONK

Map 1; 409 Broadway, Downtown; ///minus.inch.camera;
www.nudieshonkytonk.com

Named for the tailor and creator of the Nudie suit – a colorful,
rhinestone-covered suit modeled by the likes of Elvis, Cher, and
Elton John – Nudie's is part-museum, part-honky-tonk. Walls are
bedecked with glitzy, fringed stage costumes worn by country
greats, music memorabilia, and even Nudie Cohn's Cadillac El
Dorado (which is insured for an eye-watering $400,000). As for the
vibe, it's anything but museum-like. Crowds of students and
partygoers gravitate toward the seemingly endless bar (it's the
longest in Nashville, don't you know) for rounds of shots and buckets
of beers. They stay for the live music performances by young,
emerging bands, followed by late-night DJ dance parties.

Liked by the locals

"In Music City, the way to start cracking at the art of honky-tonk is on Lower Broadway. There is no other place like it in the entire country. It's where dreamers turn to legends, and where moments are turned into lasting memories."

DANIEL DONATO, AMA-NOMINATED GUITARIST
AND SINGER-SONGWRITER

LGBTQ+ Scene

In a largely conservative state, Nashville is a uniquely liberal outpost with a large LGBTQ+ community. There's still room to grow, of course, but Music City remains an inclusive place for a night out.

PECKER'S BAR AND GRILL

Map 4; 237 Hermitage Avenue, Napier; ///tight.gates.chief; www.peckersnashville.com

Where else can you see cowboys and drag queens on the same night? Pecker's is a not-so-subtly named gay bar with tons of fun events — we're talking line dancing, bingo, karaoke, and more. It's one of the most welcoming places, where locals know it's always okay to pony up to the bar in just a hoodie and jeans for friendly conversation, arrive fully dolled up for a drag show, or just drop in for Taco Tuesday.

PLAY DANCE BAR

Map 2; 1519 Church Street, North Gulch; ///coins.detail.giant; www.nashville.playdancebar.com

Imagine an entire bar of people singing the words to Lady Gaga's latest at the top of their lungs as impeccably styled drag queens do handstands on the stage. Welcome to Play, the biggest dose of dopamine you'll find on Chuch Street. A squad of footloose and fancy- free revelers adore the party bar for its spectacular drag shows and its dance room, which plays irresistible house-inflected anthems.

» Don't leave without tipping the queens and the cocktail servers. It's an absolute must (and considered a snub if you don't).

TRIBE

Map 2; 1517 Church Street, North Gulch; ///nerve.dined.class; www.tribenashville.com

Play's more relaxed counterpart, Tribe is all about socializing rather than strutting. Savor a fruity cocktail and chat to the posse of laid-back 20- and 30-somethings (you can actually hear people here, hallelujah). But don't mistake chill for boring – Tribe also hosts *RuPaul's Drag Race* viewing parties, drag appearances, and show-tune nights for when you're feeling your most extra.

Shh!

Old Glory is so much more than a reliably good cocktail joint *(p66)*. Once a month, the bar hosts a night that's all about celebrating queer bodies. The creation of drag queen and Southern belle Vidalia Anne, the GLITZ! party encourages attendees to really embrace their queerness by serving a "lewk" (literally anything goes), with a photographer on hand to capture the event. Though the night is primarily a safe space for the queer community, allies are welcome to join the fun.

LIPSTICK LOUNGE

Map 3; 1400 Woodland Street, East Nashville; ///bend.booth.desire;
www.thelipsticklounge.com

Karaoke in Nashville can be a bit fraught; caught in the wrong place and it can just be a crowd of plastered bachelor parties or singer-songwriter hopefuls trying too hard to catch the eye of local record execs. Not at Lipstick Lounge. This spot has all the welcoming vibes of your best friend's living room. Need proof? Owner Jonda regularly gets up on stage to sing soulfully to her beloved patrons, who all return the love with hoots and hollers as she hits the high notes. This iconic bar was created with the lesbian community in mind, but it's as inclusive as they come; whatever your background or story, you'll feel right at home.

» Don't leave without snapping a picture on the bench outside – it's shaped like, you guessed it, a huge pair of lips. Ask nicely and Jonda might join you.

CANVAS LOUNGE

Map 2; 1707 Church Street, North Gulch; ///most.study.fast;
www.canvasnash.com

When you're not in the mood for a long, winding line or paying a hefty cover charge, head to uber-chilled Canvas on Church Street. Here a neighborly bartender will prepare you a drink and ask about your day beneath the Moroccan lanterns, fairy lights, and neon honky-tonk signs that illuminate the cozy bar. When you're ready, sashay onto the dance floor where you'll be greeted by a genuine and fun-loving crowd – you'll probably make a new friend or two.

LGBTQ+ SCENE

For another chilled but slightly older crowd, head to LGBTQ+-friendly dive Trax in Wedgewood-Houston.

This gay bar is mainly geared toward men but everyone is invited to join the party, especially on Thursday and Sunday karaoke nights.

SUZY WONG'S HOUSE OF YUM

Map 2; 1515 Church Street, North Gulch; ///poker.glare.critic;
www.suzywongsnashville.com

Mimosas, rhinestones, avocado toast, more rhinestones – Suzy Wong's is Nashville's original drag brunch and now drag dinner. It's a staple for out-of-towners and bachelorette parties but that doesn't deter the locals, who love this spot for its delicious menu plated up with a side of glamour. Celebrity chef and Nashville native Arnold Myint serves up Asian-inspired dishes with accents of Southern cuisine like katsu chicken waffles. But the real star of the show? That's Myint's alter-ego, the hostess with the mostest Suzy Wong herself, of course.

QDP AT BASEMENT EAST

Map 3; 917 Woodland Street, East Nashville; ///rocks.edgy.strain;
www.thebasementnashville.com

The energy at pop-up QDP (or Queer Dance Party) is that of people living their best lives. Held at Basement East on the third Friday of the month, the boisterous party is one of Nashville's finest LGBTQ+ events thanks largely to its staunch mission to provide a safe space for all; check out their QDProtocol, which is based around consent, anti-racism, and accessibility.

Music Bars

In Nashville, music doesn't just belong in concert halls. Stumble into one of these intimate bars any night of the week and you're guaranteed to discover a great band covering the classics or trying out a new tune.

RUDY'S JAZZ ROOM

Map 1; 809 Gleaves Street, Downtown; ///incomes.trash.noisy; www.rudysjazzroom.com

Speakeasy-style Rudy's attracts serious talent from the jazz world (we're talking world-renowned musicians, y'all), making it the premier jazz venue in the city. With moody lighting and sublime tunes, it's little wonder that couples choose Rudy's for date night.

Shh!

A lot of Nashvillians want to keep this place hush hush but we're letting you in on the secret. Belcourt Taps is a cozy bar with lovely bohemian village vibes and live acoustic music seven nights a week (*www.belcourttaps.com*). It's the sort of place where patrons probably know someone playing, and the musicians sit among the locals after the performance.

BOWIE'S

Map 1; 174 3rd Avenue North, Downtown; ///bared.honest.open; www.bowiesnashville.com

You can make a drinking game out of how many times you'll hear "Wagon Wheel" in Downtown Nashville. But not at Bowie's, a rock 'n' roll bar named for the British music icon, where girls in bell bottoms dance to live rock covers. It feels a bit clubby, but so what? Let's dance.

THE LOCAL

Map 5; 110 28th Avenue North, West End; ///twin.scans.object; www.localnash.com

Arrive a stranger, leave a local; neighborhood darling The Local will make you feel like a Nashvillian. A haven for up-and-coming country artists, the music bar hosts folk and bluegrass bands who are carefully chosen by country-obsessed owner Geoff Reid (a songwriter himself).
» Don't leave without checking out the craft beer menu, which is dedicated to celebrating brews made here in Tennessee.

THE 5 SPOT

Map 3; 1006 Forrest Avenue, East Nashville; ///scope.colleague.homes; www.the5spot.club

You'll love this magical nook of a bar where local and some traveling musicians lay down serious notes to an appreciative audience of seasoned rockers, hipsters, soul lovers, and everyone in between. The stage hosts artists of every music genre imaginable, but it really comes alive at Sunday Night Soul and Motown Monday.

BOURBON STREET BLUES AND BOOGIE BAR

Map 1; 220 Printers Alley, Downtown; ///pencil.being.gently;
www.bourbonstreetbluesandboogiebar.com

Good times always roll at Bourbon Street, a New Orleans-themed bar that's all about soul and blues (and partial to a drop of rock, too). The Creole-style balcony affords great views of the stage, so you can comfortably watch the band play while tucking into a cup of gumbo and a rum-spiked cocktail. As for the dance floor, it's small but there's always room for another. Who said Mardi Gras is just once a year?

CITY WINERY

Map 1; 609 Lafayette Street, Downtown; ///occurs.refuse.splash;
www.citywinery.com

This glorious combination of restaurant, wine bar, and venue keeps Nashvillians coming back again and again. In winter, they huddle around the bar's candlelit tables to watch country music acts; in summer, you'll find them gathered around the patio's mini stage.

STATION INN

Map 1; 402 12th Avenue South, The Gulch; ///famous.serves.vent;
www.stationinn.com

Standing stalwart beside the high rises of the Gulch is the Station Inn, a squat, stone bar packed with all the hallmarks of Americana (think cheap beer, folding furniture, and peeling concert posters). This is a home away from home for bluegrass musicians and devotees, who have been making pilgrimages to this music mainstay for more than 40 years. It's first come, first served so get here early to secure the best seat in the city for banjo-plucking bluegrass.

THE LISTENING ROOM CAFÉ

Map 1; 618 4th Avenue South, Rutledge Hill; ///clear.caged.frogs; www.listeningroomcafe.com

Songwriters are the backbone of Nashville's music community, and they get a lot of respect here in town. Like at The Listening Room, a stripped-down setting that hosts the tradition of the "writers' round," in which a group of artists take it in turns to play an original acoustic composition. Serious music fans love this experience, sipping glasses of red and savoring every lyric, almost like a poetry reading – which in some ways it is.

B.B. KING'S

Map 1; 152 2nd Avenue North, Downtown; ///frog.ports.cans; www.bbkings.com

A night at B.B. King's feels like you're at the best wedding you've ever been to; you'll be singing along to "Celebration" with a bunch of strangers – students through to grandparents – and passing around another tray of drinks before you know it. The bar's house band is one of the best in town, with a full horn section and rotating vocalists singing all your funk and soul favorites.

» Don't leave without checking out the wall art, which showcases some of the world's most famous blues players.

Game Night

Fun is the name of the game in Nashville. Of course locals like sitting in a bar and shooting the breeze, but a bar fitted out with pinball machines, board games, and foosball tables? Now we're talking.

HEADQUARTERS BEERCADE

Map 1; 114 2nd Avenue South, Downtown; ///librarian.crown.tens; www.hq-nashville.com

Above an army of pinball machines and hockey-themed foosball tables, a big neon sign reads "Don't grow up it's a trap." Die-hard gamers live by this mantra at HQ Beercade, gathering around the vintage arcade games to compete just like they did with their brothers and sisters many moons ago. Cool events also transform the space into fantastical worlds from the movies and TV, like *Stranger Things*.

PINEWOOD SOCIAL

Map 1; 33 Peabody Street, Downtown; ///noble.translated.ripe; www.pinewoodsocial.com

Ever stayed at one place, all day long? At Pinewood, it's a given. Start your morning with coffee and a breakfast bagel, which you'll tuck into alongside digital nomads setting up shop at the library-like tables.

After that, put your feet up by one of the outdoor dipping pools before the great and the good arrive; it's around 5pm that you'll see things pick up, as groups congregate for ping pong, bowling, and karaoke. And who can blame them? This place is a playground for adults.

TWO BITS

Map 2; 1520 Demonbreun Street, Downtown; ///exam.audio.among; www.twobitsnashville.com

This little video and board game bar plays hard on the nostalgia. College students and young professionals sip frozen drinks with game-inspired names (Yoshi's Island is popular) as they battle it out at Yahtzee and Jenga. Old-school belters provide the soundtrack, with a steady stream of vintage music videos on the screens behind the bar.

» Don't leave without challenging your pals to a game on the giant Connect-4 out on the front patio.

Shh!

Yes, Mangia is a lovely Italian restaurant that specializes in family-style feasts *(www.mangia nashville.com)*. But not many realize that this Melrose spot also has a bocce ball court on its patio. The brainchild of chef Nick Pellegrino, Mangia gives diners a true taste of an evening meal in Italy: hearty food to share followed by a game of bocce ball and a dance around the table (all for a very reasonable $45). So make like an Italian and head here with your loved ones – it's a night you'll remember.

Solo, Pair, Crowd

There's always a game afoot in Music City. Meet your match and show off your game at one of these bars.

FLYING SOLO
Ready player one

Say hello to Game Terminal, the city's largest arcade, in South Nashville. Enjoy unadulterated fun on one of the 200 pinball and arcade games before grabbing some grub from the rotating food truck.

IN A PAIR
Foosball for two

It's easy to get lost in Acme *(p71)* but up on the second floor you'll find a cozy corner outfitted with old-school foosball tables. Challenge a buddy to a game in between bites of sushi from the bar.

FOR A CROWD
Bowl over the competition

Book a bowling lane or challenge your buds to a game of ping pong at Pins Mechanical Company, in North Gulch. The sprawling bar also has plenty of space to sit and chat when the competition gets a little too heated.

KUNG FU SALOON

Map 5; 1921 Division Street, Midtown; ///paints.evenly.composers;
www.kungfusaloon.com

Head inside this throwback bar for vintage arcade games, like Ms.
Pacman and Mortal Kombat, and skeeball lanes that'll take you back
to your Chuck-E-Cheese birthday in the 4th grade. Need to cool off?
Join college kids on the outdoor patio for cornhole and giant Jenga.

MELROSE BILLIARD PARLOR

Map 4; 2600 8th Avenue South #108, Melrose; ///bids.goal.keeps;
www.dirtymelrose.com

This Nashville classic has been polished up but the original
divey-ness happily remains intact. Stylish weekend warriors and
poolhall regulars pack into this joint to show off their pool, pingpong,
dart and foosball skills (or lack thereof). Head's up though: things
get hazy from 10pm when the no-smoking policy is lifted.

» Don't leave without snagging some free popcorn from the
machine – it's the perfect late-night snack.

HIFI CLYDE'S

Map 2; 1700 Church Street, North Gulch; ///vital.closes.guises;
www.hificlydesnashville.com

Boisterous groups of friends love Clyde's for its rowdy games of
ping pong, shuffleboard, and foosball. The North Gulch bar is also
a popular hang with sports fans thanks to its enormous screens –
perfect for watching Nashville's NFL or NHL teams.

Music Venues

Nashville harbors an amazing array of Goldilocks venues; not too big, and not too small, these stages are the stuff of legend. These aren't music bars, though: you've got to buy your tickets ahead of time.

THE BASEMENT

Map 4; 604 8th Avenue South #330, Melrose; ///doctor.frog.olive; www.thebasementnashville.com

Dark, gritty, and cave-like, the Basement is tucked away under the old location of celebrated record store Grimey's *(p110)*. Sure, its younger sister Basement East tends to pull the bigger bands, but we love this Melrose venue for hosting eclectic and little-known local acts who play full volume to a kooky, alternative crowd. And it's so tiny and intimate that you'll really feel like you're with the band.

CANNERY ROW

Map 1; 1 Cannery Row, Downtown; ///fool.invite.inspector; www.mercylounge.com

This one is, in fact, three venues that fit together like a Russian stacking doll of stages, each with its own personality. The tiny High Watt premieres spunky local acts looking for their big break; middle sister, Mercy Lounge, is all about touring acts and popular tribute bands (like the wonderfully named Red Not Chili Peppers); and then there's queen bee Cannery Ballroom where big names like Adele, the Alabama Shakes, and Snoop Dog have entertained the masses.

EXIT/IN

Map 5; 2208 Elliston Place, Elliston; ///ratings.themes.fats;
www.exitin.com

Exit/In is a testament to all the musicians that have come before, icons like Chuck Berry, Willy Nelson, Sharon Jones, Billy Joel, and The Ramones to name literally a few. Grungy and in your face, the music forum has been exploding the minds of music fans since 1971, though these days it mostly draws a counterculture crowd by booking indie and alternative rock acts. That's not a hard-and-fast rule though; just don't expect to find any country concerts on the schedule.

>> **Don't leave without** reading the "wall of fame," which lists everyone who has ever played here. The list is wildly impressive.

ASCEND AMPHITHEATER

Map 1; 310 1st Avenue South, Downtown; ///chat.elder.offer;
www.ascendamphitheater.com

Can't make it to Coachella? A show at Ascend is a great second-best. The open-air amphitheater books all kinds of national acts – from Beck to Jeff Beck – and it's just a block from Broadway for pre-show drinks. Opt for a lawn seat from where the city skyline rises behind the stage and the stage lights reflect off the river.

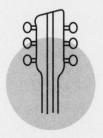

Liked by the locals

"We are beyond fortunate to have such enthusiastic music and musician-loving venue owners in Nashville. The scene is alive and thriving thanks to their support and dedication."

PHILIP SHOUSE,
NASHVILLE LOCAL AND ROCK MUSICIAN

THE BLUEBIRD CAFE

Map 5; 4104 Hillsboro Pike, Green Hills; ///stud.clock.fund;
www.bluebirdcafe.com

If one venue has defined Nashville's modern music scene, it's the Bluebird. The small strip-mall stage hosts "writers' rounds," the very events that got Garth Brooks and Taylor Swift discovered. Unsurprisingly, it's packed out with tourists, music nuts, and the occasional record exec so it's vital that you secure seats in advance.

MARATHON MUSIC WORKS

Map 2; 1402 Clinton Street, Marathon Village; ///bared.oval.valve;
www.marathonmusicworks.com

Set in an old motorworks factory, Marathon is huge and promises you and your squad tons of room to get down and dance. You won't see anyone on the Top 40 here, but that's part of the appeal; you'll be raving with the next big names in rock, hip-hop, indie, and country.

3RD & LINDSLEY

Map 1; 818 3rd Avenue South, Rutledge Hill; ///valid.bunks.later;
www.3rdandlindsley.com

For people who are into indie shows, but not into feeling squished between hundreds of people they've never met, 3rd & Lindsley is the perfect forum. Fans are seated at tables, giving all the vibes of a music bar but with bigger names and incredible cover bands performing.
» Don't leave without tuning into Nashville's independent radio station, Lightning 100, which sponsors Sunday nights at 3rd & Lindsley.

0 meters 50
0 yards 50

Public Square Park

UNION STREET

Printers Alley *was known as the "Men's Quarter" in the 19th century thanks to its glut of gambling parlors and saloons.*

UNION STREET

PRINTERS ALLEY

A nightcap at BLACK RABBIT

Pair a cocktail with a late night snack at this speakeasy, which pays homage to the past with live parlor music and vintage decor.

①

Dinner at ELLINGTON'S

Start your evening right with a decadent dinner at this elegant, mid-century style restaurant. It'll give you total *Mad Men* vibes.

BANKERS ALLEY

3RD AVENUE NORTH

④

Shake your tail feather at BOURBON STREET BLUES AND BOOGIE BAR

Swing by this New Orleans-themed bar where a live blues band is on hand to help you dance your troubles away.

②
③

Enjoy the show at SKULL'S RAINBOW ROOM

Burlesque is the main attraction at this legendary basement bar. Swirl a whiskey as you enjoy a titillating performance.

4TH AVENUE NORTH

Two original "Men's Quarter" saloon buildings (the saloons have closed) can be spotted at **210 and 212 Fourth Avenue North**.

STREET

CHURCH STREET

DOWNTOWN

A night out on
Printers Alley

Spend a lively evening in Downtown's Printers Alley, a historic passageway with a storied past and vibrant nightlife. This blink-and-you'll-miss-it street has had many incarnations over the years, from a notorious stretch of speakeasies, saloons, and nightclubs (complete with peep shows and prohibition-era parties) to a publishing hub (hence the name). Today, music spills out into the characterful alley, where old brick buildings house rowdy bars, cozy restaurants, cabaret shows, and karaoke joints — all tinged with a wonderful vintage feel.

1. Ellington's
401 Union Street, Downtown; www.ellingtons.restaurant
///human.senior.music

2. Bourbon Street Blues and Boogie Bar
220 Printers Alley, Downtown; www.bourbonstreetblues andboogiebar.com
///pencil.being.gently

3. Skull's Rainbow Room
222 Printers Alley, Downtown; www.skulls rainbowroom.com
///rush.seat.began

4. Black Rabbit
218 3rd Avenue North, Downtown; www.black rabbittn.com
///nurses.gold.lofts

 **210 and 212 Fourth Avenue North** ///stored.plots.enjoyable

OUTDOORS

Locals don't have to travel far for alfresco adventure in Nashville – they've got parks, lakes, rivers, waterfalls, and those Tennessee hills right in their backyard.

Picnic Spots

The warm Tennessee sun lures locals out to Nashville's green spaces for leisurely picnics. These gorgeous spots invite you to kick off those shoes and enjoy the slower life, just for a little while.

LOVE CIRCLE

Map 5; 330 Love Circle, Hillsboro; ///debate.evenly.span

A precarious, spiraling drive up a hill brings you to Love Circle, a panoramic viewpoint that affords stellar views of the Downtown skyline. The park itself is not much of a looker, thanks to a series of fenced-off utility transformers, but Love Circle's devoted following of high school and college kids makes it an affable place to picnic – cute dogs, nice tunes, and good laughs abound. Be warned: there's a fair share of making out that goes on, here. Ah, to be young.

RIVERFRONT PARK

Map 2; 100 1st Avenue North, Downtown; ///agreed.tunes.neon; www.nashville.gov

The Cumberland River is one of the city's most defining features, and Riverfront Park is the best place to spread out a picnic blanket and watch the water roll by beneath the city's glittering skyline. All sorts of things might pass through your periphery here – the steamboat that regularly floats up and down this stretch of the river or a wedding photoshoot on the John Seigenthaler Pedestrian Bridge (p174). Plenty of entertainment to accompany an alfresco feast.

» **Don't leave without** grabbing some pralines from Leon's, which is a 10-minute walk from the park. The candies are the perfect picnic finish.

CUMBERLAND PARK

Map 3; 592 South 1st Street, Downtown; ///guilty.money.lions; www.nashville.gov

When school's out for summer, families pack the sandwiches and juice boxes and head to Cumberland Park, across the water from Riverfront Park; follow in their footsteps and relive your own summer break. Meander around the pretty Explorer Trail, abundant with brightly colored butterflies, and stop at the park's scooped lawn for a picnic . In the height of summer, a post-lunch frolic through the park's water fountains is mandatory.

MCCABE PARK

Map 5; 101 46th Avenue North, Sylvan Park; ///soon.vague.pens; www.nashville.gov

At the heart of Sylvan Park lies McCabe Park, a community greenway that sees a conveyer belt of human activity: couples puffing on their weekly run, teenagers practicing their rollerblading skills, dog walkers swapping stories with one another, and retirees gossiping as they power walk. There's no better place for a people-watching picnic.

CHEEKWOOD

Map 6; 1200 Forrest Park Drive, Belle Meade; ///jelly.noon.dreams;
www.cheekwood.org

When locals are planning a celebratory picnic, they pack their baskets and make for Cheekwood. Inspired by 18th-century English manors, the grounds comprise an elegant garden and Georgian-style mansion, which was home to the family that owned Maxwell House Coffee before Cheekwood was opened up to the good people of Nashville. Today the estate makes a dreamy setting for a blowout lunch with loved ones, thanks to the immaculate flowerbeds, trickling water features, and striking sculptures sprinkled across the gardens. If you're looking to raise a glass over your picnic, the café sells alcoholic beverages that you can take back to your blanket.

>> Don't leave without paying a little bit more to enter the mansion and take in the artworks on display. Aside from works by the likes of Jamie Wyeth and Andy Warhol, there are pieces by local artists.

Shh!

A wild, wonderful woodland lies hidden a stone's throw from East Nashville's Shelby Park. Lockeland Springs Park might be just three acres but, boy, are those acres magical. The copse is home to natural springs (the water was bottled here in the 19th century, and you can see the ruins of the bottling plant) and little fairy gardens that are built into and around the base of tree trunks. Pack a picnic lunch and find a secret spot under the trees for a little slice of tranquility in the city.

SEVIER PARK

Map 4; 3021 Lealand Lane, 12 South; ///taker.tuned.invest; www.nashville.gov

At the very end of neighborly 12 South you'll find a little urban oasis. Every day Sevier Park sees families with strollers walking alongside the park's babbling brook, students catching up on their reading under the shade of trees, and young professionals sunbathing or playing games of frisbee. The best time to lay out a rug beside them? On a Tuesday afternoon, when a farmers' market (and, better yet, a puppy play pen) occupies the park's grassy hill. Stock up on locally grown and made picnic fare and let the afternoon drift by – someone will likely strum on a guitar while you graze.

CENTENNIAL PARK

Map 5; 2500 West End Avenue, West End; ///votes.below.family; www.nashville.gov

Long wanted to visit Greece? Centennial Park will bring you a little closer thanks to its full-scale replica of the Parthenon (p124). Yes, the structure embodies Nashville's cultural reputation as the "Athens of the South," and is home to the terrifingly large Athena Parthenos statue (we're talking 42 ft, or 13 m). But it also makes the most magnificent backdrop for a picnic, especially as it faces a large lake replete with weeping willows. So make like you're on vacation – good book, sunscreen, floppy hat – and drink in the scenery as you tuck into your picnic. After lunch, get some exercise on the park's walking trail or wander over to Musicians Corner where a local artist might well be performing for picnickers.

Wonderful Walks

*For everyone from hardy hikers to casual
strollers, weekends in Nashville are all about
donning sneakers or walking boots, being in
nature, and seeing the city from a different angle.*

STONES RIVER GREENWAY

Map 6; start at Kohl's parking lot, Donelson; ///ripe.sooner.hogs

Nashville's cycling set love to whizz along this route, which starts by
the Cumberland and snakes for 11 miles (18 km) along the offshoot
Stones River. But it's not just for wheels; locals like to stretch their legs
along the boardwalks of a Sunday afternoon. The paved path winds
beneath the arced branches of riparian trees, across rolling meadows,
and over creek beds alive with chirping frogs. The best bit? It ends at
pretty Percy Priest Lake. Good things come to those who wait (or walk).

PERCY WARNER PARK

**Map 6; Forrest Park Drive, Belle Meade; ///most.swaps.exists;
www.nashville.gov**

You'll be pleased to hear that you don't need to leave the city to find
great hiking opportunities. Take Percy Warner Park, which is stuffed
with trails – some 17 miles (27 km) worth, in fact, plus paths for a light

stroll. The 4.5-mile (7-km) Mossy Ridge Trail takes weekend walkers through wooded hills, across meadows, and around springs, while the 2.5-mile (4-km) Warner Woods Trail is popular with those looking for a short walk with killer views. A word to the wise: don't underestimate these hikes. Both require a fair bit of energy, thanks to various hills, so come with walking boots and be ready for a workout.

» **Don't leave without** walking up to the Allée overlook, near the park's Belle Meade entrance, for a wonderful view out over the city.

EDWIN WARNER PARK

Map 6; Highway 100, Belle Meade; ///goodbye.continuously.devalued; www.nashville.gov

Percy's little brother Edwin Warner (the parks were genuinely named for park commissioner brothers) is the park of choice for those who hate puffing breathlessly up a hill or lacing up hefty boots. Its clutch of shorter trails includes the 3-mile (5-km) Harpeth Woods Trail, which covers part of the original Natchez Trace Parkway (p184).

SHELBY BOTTOMS GREENWAY

Map 3; start at Shelby Bottoms Nature Center parking lot, East Nashville; ///foal.photo.claims; www.nashville.gov

Nestled along the first riverbend headed away from the city, Shelby Bottoms is a welcome urban surprise. It's got it all: wetlands, streams, open fields, and dense forest, all just five minutes from Downtown. So lace up your sneakers and enjoy an afternoon's stroll – you'll eventually connect with Stones River Greenway.

JOHN SEIGENTHALER PEDESTRIAN BRIDGE

**Map 3; entrance near 123 2nd Avenue South, Downtown;
///shirt.jabs.single**

Find out why Bob Dylan found Music City's skyline so inspiring by walking along the John Seigenthaler Pedestrian Bridge (named for the journalist and founder of *The Tennessean* newspaper). One of the longest pedestrian bridges in the world, at 3,150 ft (960 m) in length, it takes you high over the Cumberland River with a bird's-eye view of Downtown's skyscrapers and a soundtrack of music drifting up from the honky-tonks and buskers below. All this without breaking a sweat – praise be. Time your walk for sunset for a truly memorable view.

RADNOR LAKE STATE PARK

**Map 6; Otter Creek Road, Forest Hills; ///robots.regime.hardly;
www.tnstateparks.com**

One thing locals can all agree on: Radnor Lake State Park is stunning. It's little wonder that this is where music stars head for a bit of solitude between shows (Mick Jagger and Taylor Swift are both known to take a turn around the state park). And they're not the only ones; young hikers walk the 2.5-mile (4-km) trail around the lake, where families look out for fish and diving birds. To nurture the park's feeling of Zen, trail running and pets aren't allowed but, let's be honest, it's worth sacrificing the cardio blast for a peaceful walk in nature. Note the parking lot can get very crowded on beautiful days, so get there early.

» Don't leave without stopping inside the nature center at the trailhead to learn about the park's preservation efforts.

Liked by the locals

"The pedestrian bridge is such a magical place where you can watch the sun set behind the city skyline and walk over to the bustling streets of Downtown. It's the best skyline view in the city."

SARA BILL,
NASHVILLE WEDDING PHOTOGRAPHER

Alfresco Fitness

*All that hot chicken and gravy-soaked biscuits can take
their toll. The good news? Nashville has got so many
ways to work out while also enjoying the city, making
alfresco exercise possible every day of the week.*

CAPITOL STEPS WORKOUT

Map 2; 600 Dr. M.L.K. Jr Boulevard, Downtown; ///zooms.stops.rich

The best workouts are free, right? This is certainly the mentality of
James Crumlin, a local lawyer living a double life as a triathlon and
running coach. Twice a week (on Mondays and Thursdays), the
fitness fiend leads a band of locals up and down the highest hill in
the city, stopping for burpees, lunges, and ab exercises. It's hard work,
no doubt, but James is on hand to cheer you on.

STAND-UP PADDLE BOARDING

**Map 6; start at Hamilton Creek Recreation Area, Percy Priest Lake;
///crooner.catty.remotely; www.nashvillepaddle.com**

We've got the perfect workout for a hot day in the city. Yep, it's
stand-up paddle boarding, which has had locals falling hard and
fast – literally. Join parties of young people working their core as
they navigate Percy Priest Lake and chat as you paddle alongside

them (or try to – concentration is key). Looking for something a little more chill? Nashville Paddle Company runs yoga paddle classes where sun salutations are practiced atop paddle boards on the Percy Priest Lake. What could possibly go wrong?

» Don't leave without asking about the completely magical full-moon paddle where, once a month, star-struck attendees paddle beneath the night sky (prior experience is recommended).

NASHVILLE FRONTRUNNERS

Map 2; start at 1707 Church Street, North Gulch; ///most.study.fast; www.frontrunners.org

Every Monday, at 6.30pm, this friendly LGBTQ+ running club meet at Canvas Lounge *(p150)* to take a new route through Nashville's glittering Downtown, breathlessly catching up on the week's news and waving at passersby. Out-of-towners are just as welcome as long-time locals, and you don't have to run if you don't want to – walkers are likewise invited. Can't make Monday? The club also meets at Lipstick Lounge *(p150)* on Thursdays.

Try it!
AERIAL ACROBATICS

Want to emulate Cirque du Soleil? Learn the dynamic skills of the swing, catch, and drop at the Nashville School for the Aerial Arts *(www.nashvilleaerialarts.com)*, a tented center with all the trapeze trimmings.

Solo, Pair, Crowd

Whether you prefer to exercise alone, in a pair, or en masse, there's a fun workout for you.

FLYING SOLO

Join a jog

Make some new friends while getting in your miles with the Dirtbags Trail Run Club. Meet at 6pm on Thursdays at the Deep Well entrance of Percy Warner Park for a run off the beaten path.

IN A PAIR

A cycle for two

Rent a couple of bicycles from one of Nashville B-Cycle's kiosks and cruise alongside the Cumberland on the Shelby Bottoms Greenway.

FOR A CROWD

Set and spike by the Parthenon

Gather your crew and head to Centennial Park for some sand volleyball in the park's outdoor courts. The Parthenon provides a beautiful backdrop for a post-game picnic on the hill.

KAYAK DOWN THE CUMBERLAND

Map 3; start at Cumberland Park, 592 South 1st Street, Downtown;
///fetch.quite.bolts

A workout with gorgeous, uninterrupted city views? Now we're talking. Follow the lead of locals in-the-know who hop in single and tandem kayaks to admire Music City from a new perspective (bar the odd steamboat), all while trying not to fall in after a wobble.

WELLNESS 360 AT CHEEKWOOD

Map 6; 1200 Forrest Park Drive, Belle Meade; ///jelly.noon.dreams;
www.cheekwood.org

Suffice to say we could all use a little (or a lot) more calm these days, so the Wellness 360 program at Cheekwood (p170) should sit high on anyone's list. Classes cover activities like forest bathing, meditation, yoga, and mindfulness, all in the tranquil Cheekwood grounds.

SWIM IN PERCY PRIEST LAKE

Map 6; Anderson Road Recreation Area, Percy Priest Lake;
///crisp.hogging.wobbling

When it's feeling hot hot hot, locals have one form of exercise in mind: a cooling dip. Boisterous groups of guys and gals park up at Percy Priest Lake for a day of swimming off one of the designated beaches. Okay, it's more splashing about than breaststroke, and there's often a BBQ involved. But we all need a bit of motivation, right?

» Don't leave without exploring the trails of the adjacent Long Hunter State Park, which has some hidden swimming spots of its own.

Nearby Getaways

Of course Nashvillians love their city, but sometimes a change of scene is just the ticket. Luckily, Music City has various tempting day trips right on its doorstep.

SOUTH CUMBERLAND STATE PARK

2-hour drive from the city; www.tnstateparks.com

Soaring sandstone cliffs, perfectly clear streams, and waterfalls tumbling into shaded lagoons: for a taste of Eden, South Cumberland State Park ticks all the boxes. At least the locals certainly think so. Come the weekend, work-weary Nashvillians pining for a dose of nature flock to the state park, picnic and beach towel in tow, and set up camp by one of the park's 12 stunning falls.

MAMMOTH CAVE NATIONAL PARK

1.5-hour drive from the city; www. nps.gov

We know, Nashville can be pretty uncomfortable in summer (oh the humidity), especially if you've arrived from cooler climes. And that's why a lot of locals drive across to Kentucky to spend the day at Mammoth Cave National Park, staying cool in the caves (you might need a layer, in all seriousness). Follow the herd and wind your way around the incredible cave system – the world's longest, don't you know. All the dripping stalagmites are like something from a scene in *Star Wars*.

» Don't leave without joining one of the spelunking trips, which take you deep into the hidden nooks and crannies of the cave system. Claustrophobes, you'll want to sit this one out.

LONG HUNTER STATE PARK

45-minute drive from the city; www.tnstateparks.com

It might sound strange, but it's worth exploring Long Hunter State Park after it's rained. Why? You'll spot all sorts of amphibious wildlife hopping along the path as you stroll around the ancient parkland, and you'll have the place to yourself. Long Hunter might wrap around the eastern side of popular Percy Priest Lake but the state park feels light-years away from the hullabaloo of Music City. Perfect for when you're craving a bit of calm.

HARPETH RIVER STATE PARK

30-minute drive from the city; www.tnstateparks.com

Nashville's locals love the Harpeth River, a shallow tributary of the Cumberland. Here in the state park, the waterway provides a 40-mile (65-km) stretch with nine drop-in spots for kayaks and canoes. College kids race for imaginary finish lines, couples seek out quiet expanses to drift along in their tandem kayak, and parents try to keep canoes upright as their kids squeal delightedly. No kayak? No problem. Local outfits like Foggy Bottom and Music City Kayaks offer all-day rentals for great prices.

PINSON MOUNDS STATE ARCHAEOLOGICAL PARK

2-hour drive from the city; www.tnstateparks.com

This sprawling archaeological site features an incredible 15 mounds created by Native American groups during the Woodland Period, roughly 1,500 years ago. History buffs can wind through the mounds on several trails, and dig deeper at the park museum. The park also hosts annual activities to celebrate Native American culture and prehistory – check the calendar to see what's coming up.

ASHLAND CITY

30-minute drive from the city; www.ashlandcitytn.gov

It's official: Ashland City is *the* new place to hang. Linked to Nashville by the Cumberland, the town feels gloriously rural with uninterrupted country views left, right, and center. During the day, locals potter about running errands; come night, they descend upon Riverview Restaurant and Marina for its famous fried catfish. Add to the mix a daily farmers' market and annual music festival and it's little wonder that Music City's young professionals are putting down roots here.

» **Don't leave without** stopping off at Beaman Park to stretch your legs. The wonderfully rugged expanse has a number of hiking trails.

SHORT MOUNTAIN DISTILLERY

1-hour drive from the city; www.shortmountaindistillery.com

Drink moonshine (the totally legal kind) from a mason jar at Short Mountain Distillery, a rustic small batch distillery just an hour outside of Nashville. Some spirits are organic and made with natural spring water, others are brewed with tea – because what's more Southern than tea and moonshine put together? The distillery runs tours and also has a great on-site farm-to-table restaurant, perfect for pulling up a rocking chair and looking out over what Southerners like to call "God's country" (think rolling hills, lush trees, and nothing but nature in every direction).

Try it!
MOONSHINE MIXOLOGY

Moonshine was meant to be drunk with mixers, did you know? Learn the art of making moonshine cocktails with the good people of Short Mountain before sampling your creations out on the porch.

BLEDSOE CREEK STATE PARK

1-hour drive from the city; www.tnstateparks.com

Hugging the shore of Old Hickory Lake, Bledsoe is particularly popular with hikers who enjoy exploring the hilly forest meadows. The park used to be hunting grounds for regional Native nations, and remnants of old walls can be seen throughout the park.

JACK DANIELS DISTILLERY

1.5-hour drive from the city; www.jackdaniels.com

Let's set this straight off the bat: no Music City local drives out to the Jack Daniels Distillery unless they have an insistent friend visiting from out-of-town. Nothing against JD – it's America's best-selling spirit, after all – so what's the issue? Well, the Tennessee whiskey is strangely produced in a dry county (Lynchburg, to be specific), meaning you can't drink on site. Still, that doesn't stop thousands of whiskey-lovers from visiting the distillery every year to stock up on bottles to take home.

ROCK ISLAND STATE PARK

2-hour drive from the city; www.tnstateparks.com

This exceptional little state park centers around the rocky Caney Fork Gorge, located right below the Great Falls Dam. Waterfalls – big and small – line the gorge, and shallow pools and crevices are home to enchanting ecosystems of ferns, flowers and frogs (and more). Embrace your inner naturalist with your most intrepid pals and hit the Eagle and Blue Hole trails, which take you across streams and underneath gentle sheets of waterfall spray. Thinking of a camping trip? Rock Island makes a crackerjack base for exploring this watery wonderland.

NATCHEZ TRACE PARKWAY

30-minute drive from the city; www.nps.gov

Don't confuse this one with Natchez Trace State Park in Western Tennessee. The parkway – a well-trodden trading route established by Native Americans – stretches for some 440 miles (710 km) from Nashville, Tennessee to Natchez, Mississippi. Picking up the main stretch in Pasquo, just outside of Nashville, locals love to drive the gloriously leafy route in the fall when trees burst into fiery auburn hues. Windows down, playlist on full volume – it's hard to beat.

» Don't leave without stopping at the turnoff for Burns Branch to enjoy a beautiful creek-side picnic beneath the shade of trees.

FIERY GIZZARD TRAIL

2-hour drive from the city

Backpackers agree that Fiery Gizzard is a truly rewarding hike – and we can see why. This 13-mile (21-km) out-and-back gives stunning scenery (think rushing creeks, cascading waterfalls, and ancient rock gardens) and a proper workout thanks to the tough terrain. While serious hikers kitted out in the latest walking gear go the whole hog, plenty of weekend strollers prefer to keep things simple, taking the shorter Fiery Gizzard Trail up to Raven's Point, where they swoon over the views of the Cumberland Plateau.

NEAREST GREEN DISTILLERY

1-hour drive from the city; www.unclenearest.com

We love this place. Nearest Green Distillery opened its doors in 2020 and, with it, made CEO Fawn Weaver the first African American woman to lead a major spirits brand. The distillery itself has won numerous awards and honors the legacy of Nathan "Nearest" Green, the country's first Black master distiller, who taught Jack Daniels (yes, Jack Daniels) how to make whiskey. In a nutshell: you can't pass this one by.

DAVID CROCKETT STATE PARK

2-hour drive from the city; www.tnstateparks.com

Beautiful and complex, this state park shouldn't be overlooked. Once the homestead of frontiersman, politician, and folk hero Davy Crockett, whose exploits have often (erroneously) been memorialized in movies, shows, and music, it also harbors a piece of history that documents one of the country's most horrific human rights abuses: the

Shh!

Driving to and fro David Crockett State Park? Why not stop off in the nearby city of Lawrenceburg, where you'll find a number of Amish stores provisioned with cheese, soaps, honeys, and more – all lovingly made by the local Amish community. Fill your shoes with suitcase-friendly goodies to take back home with you.

Trail of Tears. Today's hiking trails crisscross the path on which thousands of Native Americans were forced to tread as they left their ancestral homes. So many people passed through here that the trail is literally indented into the earth, sloped on either side by their footfall.

CUMMINS FALLS STATE PARK

2-hour drive from the city; www.tnstateparks.com

If state parks were people, Cummins Falls would be the influencer. Like scenes from social media, couples canoodle in the swimming hole at its base, the bravehearted jump into its icy waters, and groups of friends relax and take photographs on the rocks around the pool. Please don't be fooled, though: sturdy shoes are an absolute must around here; it's a 1.5-mike (2-km) hike up to the 75-ft (23-m) waterfall, after all. And you need a $6 permit to gain access.

OLD STONE FORT STATE ARCHAEOLOGICAL PARK

1.5-hour drive from the city; www.tnstateparks.com

On the summer solstice, Nashvillians and their fellow Tennesseans gravitate toward Old Stone Fort. They follow the trail that traces the wall of the structure (believed to have been built a whopping 1,500–2,000 years ago) before reaching the original entrance. Here, they huddle together to watch the sun rise over the horizon, just as Native Americans did millennia ago. It's an electrifying experience.

>> Don't leave without talking to a park ranger, who will give you the full lowdown on the park's lengthy history.

An afternoon in
Centennial Park

Welcome to Nashville's favorite pleasure garden, where locals tuck into sociable picnics, relax with a book, play volleyball tournaments, or catch one of the city's many festivals. It might look like the park has long been here but Centennial Park was in fact landscaped for the 1897 Tennessee Centennial Exposition. Lakes, performing arts centers, and the life-sized replica of The Parthenon were built for people to enjoy – and they've been doing it ever since. Gather your pals and find out what all the fuss is about.

1. Three Brothers Coffee
2813 West End Avenue, West End; www.threebrothers.coffee
///aspect.certified.smiled

2. Centennial Park Walking Trail
///laser.remedy.admits

3. Lake Watauga
///type.retire.appear

4. The Parthenon
2500 West End Avenue, West End
///animal.flap.dated

5. The Local
110 28th Avenue North, West End; www.localnash.com
///twin.scans.object

Centennial Art Center ///order.brass.spaces

Centennial Dog Park

28TH AVENUE NORTH

PARTHENON AVENUE

WEST END

The **Centennial Art Center** was originally a swimming pool. It closed in the 60s when Black activists fought for their right to use it.

PARK PLAZA

Lake Watauga

Loop around
LAKE WATAUGA

Keep walking until you get to Lake Watauga, a beautiful pond with whimsical bridges and weeping willows. Sit and admire the scenery.

3

25TH AVENUE NORTH

MIDTOWN

4

Marvel at
THE PARTHENON

Stop to admire Nashville's incredible, full-scale replica of Athens' Parthenon. Hot out? Catch some shade and culture inside.

PARTHENON AVENUE

28TH AVENUE NORTH

27TH AVENUE NORTH

2

Join the
CENTENNIAL PARK
WALKING TRAIL

The walking trail passes loads of the park's best spots. Look out for the Bandshell where, if you're lucky, you might overhear a Shakespeare play.

Centennial Park

31ST AVENUE NORTH

POSTON AVENUE

Rest up at
THE LOCAL

5

Treat yourself to a sandwich and brew (and maybe some live music) on the patio at this local favorite – you've earned it.

WEST END AVENUE

TRACE

NATCHEZ TRACE

1

Get caffeinated at
THREE BROTHERS COFFEE

Pick up an iced coffee from this cute coffee shop and head across the street to enter the park.

0 meters 250
0 yards 250

With a little research and preparation, this city will feel like a home away from home. Check out these websites to ensure a healthy, safe stay in Nashville.

Nashville
DIRECTORY

SAFE SPACES

Nashville is known for being a liberal and bighearted city, but should you feel uneasy or want to find your community, there are spaces catering to different sexualities, demographics, and religions.

www.blackownednashville.com
A curated online guide to Nashville's Black-owned businesses.

www.casaazafran.org
A Hispanic community center acting as a welcoming cultural space for all.

www.collective615.com
The city's first co-working space specifically for local and visiting women.

www.icntn.org
A mosque and center for both local and visiting Muslims to pray and connect.

www.pflagnashville.org
Local division of PFLAG, an organization supporting the LGBTQ+ community.

www.southernersonnewground.org
An LGBTQ+ network in the South.

HEALTH

Health care in the US isn't free, so it's important to take out comprehensive health insurance for your visit. If you do need medical assistance, there are many pharmacies and hospitals across the city.

www.nashville.gov/Health-Department.aspx
Metro Public Health Department offers advice and a list of the city's health centers.

www.walgreens.com
Store locator showing 24-hour and late-night Walgreens pharmacies.

www.plannedparenthood.org
Nonprofit organization providing sexual health care for all.

www.vumc.org
Vanderbilt University Medical Center, Nashville's major hospital and emergency department.

TRAVEL SAFETY ADVICE
Before you travel – and while you're here – always keep tabs on the latest regulations in Nashville, and the US.

www.accuweather.com
Weather forecasts and advisories, including hurricane alerts.

www.cdc.gov
National public health institute offering disease prevention and guidance.

www.nashville.gov
COVID-19 news and advice from the Metro Government of Nashville & Davidson County, Tennessee.

www.sacenter.org
Statewide sexual assault crisis center and hotline.

www.tnstateparks.com
Safety information for local state parks.

www.travel.state.gov
Latest travel safety information from the US government.

ACCESSIBILITY
Nashville has come a long way when it comes to accessibility, though some older parts of town can prove tricky for wheelchair users. These resources will help make your journeys go smoothly.

www.acb.org
National organization providing resources and support to blind and partially sighted people.

www.bridgesfordeafandhh.org
Local nonprofit providing information and interpreting services.

www.empowertennessee.org
A center for independent living that provides a comprehensive list of accessible destinations in Nashville.

www.traillink.com
Highlights wheelchair-accessible trails in and around Nashville.

www.vkc.vumc.org/vkc/pathfinder
The Tennessee Disability Pathfinder, Vanderbilt University's database of support services across the state.

ABOUT THE ILLUSTRATOR

Mantas Tumosa

*Creative designer and illustrator Mantas
moved from his home country of Lithuania
to London back in 2011. By day, he's busy
creating bold, minimalistic illustrations
that tell a story – such as the gorgeous
cover of this book. By night, he's dreaming
of adventures away, catching up on the
basketball, and cooking Italian food
(which he can't get enough of).*

Main Contributors
Bailey Freeman, Kristen Shoates
Senior Editor Lucy Richards
Senior Designer Tania Gomes
Project Art Editor Ankita Sharma
Editor Elspeth Beidas
Proofreader Kathryn Glendenning
Senior Cartographic Editor Casper Morris
Cartography Manager Suresh Kumar
Cartographer Ashif
Jacket Designer Tania Gomes
Jacket Illustrator Mantas Tumosa
Senior Production Editor Jason Little
Senior Production Controller Stephanie McConnell
Managing Editor Hollie Teague
Managing Art Editor Bess Daly
Art Director Maxine Pedliham
Publishing Director Georgina Dee

First edition 2022

Published in Great Britain by Dorling Kindersley Limited,
DK, One Embassy Gardens, 8 Viaduct Gardens,
London SW11 7BW.

The authorised representative in the EEA is
Dorling Kindersley Verlag GmbH. Arnulfstr. 124,
80636 Munich, Germany.

Published in the United States by DK Publishing,
1450 Broadway, Suite 801, New York, NY 10018.

Copyright © 2022 Dorling Kindersley Limited
A Penguin Random House Company
22 23 24 25 10 9 8 7 6 5 4 3 2 1

The publishers cannot accept responsibility for any consequences arising from
the use of this book, nor for any material on third party websites, and cannot
guarantee that any website address in this book will be a suitable source of
travel information.

A CIP catalog record for this book is available from the British Library.

A catalog record for this book is available from the Library of Congress.

ISSN: 1542 1554
ISBN: 978 0 2415 2423 7

Printed and bound in China.

www.dk.com

FSC
www.fsc.org
MIX
**Paper from
responsible sources**
FSC™ C018179

This book was made with Forest
Stewardship Council™ certified
paper – one small step in DK's
commitment to a sustainable future.
For more information go to
www.dk.com/our-green-pledge

A NOTE FROM DK EYEWITNESS

The world is fast-changing and it's keeping us folk at
DK Eyewitness on our toes. We've worked hard to ensure
that this edition of Nashville Like a Local is up-to-date and
reflects today's favourite places but we know that standards
shift, venues close, and new ones pop up in their place. So, if
you notice something has closed, we've got something
wrong or left something out, we want to hear about it.
Please drop us a line at travelguides@dk.com